ABOUT THE AUTHOR

Craig MacDonald has written three books about United States history. He was a U.S. history honor student at San Jose State University where he graduated Phi Kappa Phi in 1971. Since then he has been a staff writer on *The San Diego Union*.

MacDonald has received several honors for his writing, including the J. William McCormack Journalism Scholarship, and a J. C. Penney-University of Missouri Consumer Affairs Reporting Award. In 1975 he was nominated for a Pulitzer Prize by *The San Diego Union* for an investigative series he wrote with another reporter on the energy crisis.

LEATHER 'N LEAD

An Anthology of Desperadoes in the Far West
1820-1920

By
CRAIG MACDONALD

Boston
BRANDEN PRESS
Publishers

To Doug, who catches bad guys, and
To my sister Sue, who caught Doug

ACKNOWLEDGMENTS

A special thanks goes to Mrs. Marion Welliver, former director of the Nevada Historical Society in Reno,* who, along with her capable assistants Douglas B. MacDonald, Jan Sterling, and Eslie Cann, have served me faithfully during my many visits there. Thanks also to John Townley, present director of the Nevada Historical Society, for making his files available to me.

My gratitude also goes to Mrs. Irene Neasham, former president of the California Historical Society and former director of the Wells Fargo History Room in San Francisco, and to her assistant, Esther Schenk, for the hours they have put up with me going through their files, records, and rare books.

Thanks also to the staffs of: Bancroft Library, University of California at Berkeley; California Room, San Jose Main Public Library; Nevada State Museum, Carson City; Nevada State Library, Carson City; Summerfield Room, Getchell Library, and MacKay School of Mines, both at the University of Nevada at Reno; Northeastern Nevada Museum; Washoe County Library, Reno; San Jose State College University Library; and California State Library, Sacramento.

The staffs at the California Room of the San Diego Library, and at the California State University at San Diego also provided considerable help.

The following individuals gave me unlimited help and encouragement on this project: William Knyvett, editor of *Desert Magazine;* Eugene Ciechanowski, Sunday editor, *The San Diego Union;* Dr. and Mrs. Franklin MacDonald, Douglas and Susan Bergtholdt, Dolores Spurgeon, and Irene Epstein.

From these individuals, libraries, and archives the author has been able to get numerous primary sources. Old journals, diaries, newspaper clippings, and unpublished theses have been made readily available to me, and are quoted from in this manuscript.

Newspapers encountered at these institutions include: the *Bellview Self-Cocker, San Jose Daily Mercury, Redding Repub-*

lican, Shasta Courier, San Francisco Examiner, Inyo Register, Eureka Daily Sentinel, Las Vegas Review, Los Angeles Times, San Francisco Alta, San Francisco Call, San Jose Mercury-News, Borax Miner, Reese River Reveille, Sonora Union Democrat, Nevada State Journal, Fresno Morning Republican, Territorial Enterprise, Santa Barbara Press, San Francisco Chronicle, San Jose Herald, Santa Cruz Sentinel, Santa Cruz Surf, Watsonville Pajaronian, the Yreka Union, Placerville Mountain-Democrat, Grass Valley Nugget, and the *Auburn Journal.*

*retired, December 1971.

CONTENTS

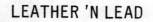

LEATHER 'N LEAD

FOREWORD

Men were tried in the crucible of the West. Some emerged with the temper of their characters stamped true by their records. Others emerged flawed. In the patterns of civilized Eastern living, the flaw had been glossed over and concealed. But in the crucible of Western crises, demanding true, resolute character, the flaw stood out, marking and distorting the false and ultimately destroying the weak.

The oft-repeated aphorism, "Man's character is his fate," stands as the measure of men in the West. Some came to measure themselves. Would they come up to taw? When they were called, would they be there? Often they did not know. In the West, they found out. Some, of course, drifted West, escaping the demands of the disciplined patterns of civilized life, unaware that their flaws would be even more marked where men had to be men.

Man's character, however, did not guarantee success. If true, it merely guaranteed respect. In the words of Edwin Arlington Robinson, a man often emerged "A valiant armor of scarred hopes outworn." Man endured life. He died, and was soon forgotten, but if he had done his bit, he contributed to the significant expansion of the nation.

In contrast with the many nameless and unsung were those who were flawed and distorted. Their natures were as various as their flaws. Greed, excitement, the sadistic desire to hurt, the psychotic desire to kill, the thrill of duplicity and deceit, all were motives. As various as their motives were their final destinies. Some were hanged without further ado; others were pardoned; some served time in prison and were the better for it; some even reversed their roles and became officers of the law.

Variety, then, characterizes the true tales in "Leather 'n Lead," a variety of flaws, of motives, of effects ranging from humor and irony to tragedy.

Given a range of mankind in an expanding environment, there will always be those who deceive, connive, rob, and murder. Eventually in the crucible, they will be sloughed and the men of true character will remain.

San Jose, California   FRANKLIN MACDONALD, PHD.

PREFACE

Leather 'n Lead is an anthology of true stories about more than fifty-five desperadoes in the Far West between 1820-1920.

The lives of these mostly unheard-of outlaws, male and female, were unearthed and pieced together by the author during a seven year investigation of archives, libraries and museums in the West.

Many of these characters came either to California's Mother Lode or to Nevada's Comstock Lode in hopes of getting rich quick.

A San Francisco newspaper editor wrote: "They came here with this hope and it takes but a few short weeks to dispel it. They are disappointed; their impatient desire for the attainment of speedy wealth seems to have no prospect for gratification.

"Temptations are about them on every hand. They drink and they gamble. They associate with men who, in their eastern homes would be shunned by them as the worst of their kind. They forget the admonitions of their mothers and sisters, given them at parting. They forget the purity of their early youth, the hopes of their riper manhood. They sink lower and lower, until they become thieves, robbers and desperadoes."

Many books covering the era 1820-1920 overlook these men and women, who, though a hazard to the environment, played an important role in molding society.

As Mark Twain once wrote, "To attempt a portrayal of that era and leave out the blood and carnage, would be like portraying Mormondom and leaving out polygamy."

San Diego, California   CRAIG MacDONALD

13

I

JOHN ALLEN
His Business Was Full of Close Shaves

John Allen was one of the better-liked barbers in Shasta, California during the 1860's. Not only did he give an exceptionally good haircut, but he was a fine conversationalist who knew where all the best fishing holes and hunting spots were. Allen was also the target of single ladies affections, since he reportedly "danced like an angel" and was admirably endowed with good looks.

At five-foot-seven, he had gray eyes, reddish-brown hair, fair complexion and a smooth manner of talk that swooned many a girl off her feet. To frost the cake, Allen, the son of a Protestant minister, could play a guitar and sing romantic songs in English, Spanish and Mexican.

However, there was one characteristic which really set Allen apart from the typical barber in Shasta. John Allen was loaded with money. He always wore the finest clothes, rode the best horses and lived in the top boarding house in town. Yet nobody ever questioned the reason a barber was able to live better than everyone else.

Besides cutting hair, John had several other occupations which kept him fitted in the style he desired. John Allen was California's most versatile outlaw. In his double life he stole horses, rustled cattle and held up stages and lone travellers.

There were many horse thefts in Northern California in the 1860's, but John Allen never came under suspicion until one day when he was caught red-handed, in Tehama, with three stolen horses. As he made a dash for freedom, the range cowboy who had surprised him cut loose with a double-barreled shotgun.

Allen had a close shave but miraculously escaped injury. The cowhand later said, "He shook my bullets from his coat like a duck sheds water." Another cowbuster, who witnessed the incident, told authorities, "When the bullets hit him they sounded like rocks thrown on a tin roof."

15

Thus Allen was tagged "Sheet-Iron Jack" by lawmen, a name which would stay with him throughout his lawless years.

The Sheriff of Tehama County quickly formed a posse that went in search of the horse thief who was an unfamiliar face in these parts. Treading on a stiff prison sentence, Sheet-Iron Jack joined the posse and provided guitar entertainment while they rode throughout the valley.

As the lawmen sat around the campfire that night, Sheet-Iron cocked his rifle, collected the posse's guns, forced them to tie each other up, relieved them of their valuables and rode off on a fresh horse, but not before thanking them for their hospitality.

Following this event, Sheet-Iron's description became well known in the Tehama as well as Shasta areas, as he continued to hold up lone travelers without wearing a disguise.

Ironically, his victims always testified that the outlaw was very polite and even amusing as he relieved them of their money.

Enjoying his successful ventures too much, Sheet-Iron became cocky and careless as he turned to the bottle. One evening, while full of spirits, he stopped at a Shasta dancehall, and, holding the hall at gunpoint, demanded to dance with his old girlfriends who had long since married. His obsession with beautiful women led him to force a local craftsman to tattoo scantily dressed women on the badman's forearms.

Jack's ability to evade the law came to an end one brisk December night when he came staggering out of a house of ill repute and fell unconscious in the street, "drunk to the gills." The Shasta County Sheriff discovered the Wanted man; and Sheet-Iron was hauled off to the pokey, from which he was soon sentenced to a couple of years in San Quentin Prison.

On his way to San Quentin, the stage in which Sheet-Iron was riding became victim of a holdup. The driver and messenger were shot, prompting the flare-up of Jack's temper. The *Shasta Courier* reported, "Jack cussed the robbers until the very air smelled like brimstone, and small streaks of lightning flashed from his mouth and played fiery circles around his head.

"Sheet-Iron said it was an unmitigated outrage that a man could not be permitted to travel over Shasta County territory, especially when he was on his way to work for the interest of the state, without having his life endangered by shots fired by murderous highwaymen."

Fortunately for Sheet-Iron, his lawyer found a legal technicality after he had served five months behind bars. As he was sent back to Shasta for a re-trial, Jack took advantage of a napping guard and stole the guard's horse.

While escaping to the wilds of Tehama County, he encountered a German greenhorn along the road who had been "done in" by a fast talking, swindler-blacksmith named Frank Phillips. Sheet-Iron, who himself had at one time been cheated by Phillips, gladly payed the blacksmith an unexpected visit.

Jack gave the taller crook a thrashing he would not soon forget. For some still unexplained reason, Sheet-Iron gave the horse and money back to the thankful greenhorn.

Evidentally bored with doing a good deed, Sheet-Iron turned from his old trade of horse stealing to stage robbing. He held up more stages in the Shasta area than did Black Bart in 1876.

Teaming up with two other prisoners "on leave," Jack held up the Redding Stage twice on a sharp, steep bend outside of Redding. They then robbed the Yreka coach of $2,000. But as is the case with criminals, Sheet-Iron was tracked down—after his horse lost a shoe—and he once again was sentenced to San Quentin, this time for twenty-four years.

However, as before, Sheet-Iron Jack lucked out. In 1882, Governor George C. Perkins declared that Allen had been convicted on insufficient evidence and on June 25, 1883 Sheet-Iron left prison with the warden's advice "to leave the state and never come back."

17

Jack did not pay much attention to advice, and he started a new illegal occupation—cattle rustling. Sheet-Iron was a successful rustler in the Northern California area, but he grew tired of the business—after all, it was hard work gathering up other peoples cattle—so he went back to his real love—horse "borrowing."

Despite his many years in the trade, Sheet-Iron Jack's knowledge regarding a horses' monetary worth was far from superb. He was arrested after selling a $500 horse for $75. The suspicious buyer knew that something was not on the up and up, and notified authorities who arrested the fugitive.

The arrest took place in April, 1884, in a Tehama saloon where Sheet-Iron had "watered his whistle" a bit too much-thus allowing the bartender to "get the drop on him." The Tehama Sheriff had the pleasure of arresting Jack for the final time.

The *Redding Republican* noted in an article on the affair, "If Sheet-Iron Jack was arrested because he sold a $500 horse for $75, we think his arrest was perfectly justifiable."

The convicting evidence in the case was a slip of paper, a receipt for a horse, on which Sheet-Iron had foolishly signed his name.

Following a ten-year term in Folsom Prison, Sheet-Iron Jack took back his real name, John Allen, and left jail for good. The colorful chapter of California's most versatile outlaw had drawn to a close.

Allen finally "saw the light" and subscribed to the belief that "crime don't pay." He became a respected citizen of Whiskeytown, north of Redding, and secured a legal job as the foreman of a crew which, oddly enough, rounded up wild horses in California.

John Allen had both given and received many close shaves in his double life as a barber-outlaw. To be able to peacefully live out his days after such a career is remarkable indeed, considering that horse thieves in the Far West

18

almost always ended up swinging uncomfortably from trees.

But then again no other horse thief was named Sheet-Iron Jack.

II

CHARLES BANKS
Sticky Fingers Put Him in Isolation

When one thinks of outlaws, the image of a murderer, bank robber, stage highwayman, train robber or burglar comes to mind. Often times, however, the most successful, financially rewarded, and hardest to catch outlaw is the embezzler. These men usually work several years—doing an admirable job—for a respected business, before absconding with the company's funds.

A true case in point is that of Charles Wells Banks, alias "J. Scard," who evaded capture following one of the biggest embezzlements in San Francisco History.

Banks was the distinguished, dependable chief cashier of Wells Fargo Bank in San Francisco. Without a doubt he was considered by his superiors to be one of the most trusted executives the Bank ever had.

He was very popular among his fellow employees and was a member in the discrete Knights Templar, the Bohemian Club, the Union Club and the San Francisco Art Association. Charles was also an avid science enthusiast and owned the first oil-immersed microscope on the Pacific Coast.

Naturally it came as quite a shock to all who knew Mr. Banks when Charles disappeared, on November 1, 1886, with reportedly over $100,000. Famed Wells Fargo Detective James B. Hume was called in on the case; and much was learned about the other life lived by the handsome cashier.

It came out that Banks was the owner of a Napa County vineyard, had a home in Oakland, as well as in San Francisco, and was, of all things, the proprietor of a seven-girl house of easy virtue on the corner of Pine and Montgomery Streets in San Francisco. Upon investigation it was suspected that he had been stealing large bills over a fourteen-year period, and that Charles gambled heavily on the stock market.

Within a week "Wanted" posters appeared throughout

the city, asking about the location of the forty-seven-year-old, five-foot-eight, 145-pound gentleman. Wells Fargo offered a $1,000 reward for the arrest of Charles who was described as having "black, slightly grey thick curly hair and small, cold grey, glance quick and comprehensive eyes." He was also called "A first class accountant; quick at counting coin and notes."

The capable Hume learned that Banks was using an alias —"J. Scard," and had rented a room on Post Street where he shaved off his beard following the embezzlement. Further tracing brought Hume to Captain John Berude of the ship, *City of Papeete* which took "J. Scard" to Tahiti via Australia. The Wells Fargo investigator also learned that "Scard" went from Tahiti to Rarotonga, the main island of the Cook Islands, Southwest of Tahiti.

Hume's men traced Banks to that island but they could not force the criminal to return to San Francisco, since "J. Scard" had been appointed auditor and government registrar of the Cook Islands in 1891.

Realizing that Banks was out of reach, Hume decided to make life as miserable as possible for the outlaw. He sent "Wanted" posters throughout the South Pacific so that Banks dared not set foot outside the Cook Islands.

Though rumors got back to Hume saying what a terrible, suffering life Banks was living, it was later learned (upon the discovery of three of Banks' diaries) that the greatest embezzler in Wells Fargo History was living a respectable, businesslike existence on the Cook Islands.

Charles Wells Banks, alias "J. Scard," died at Avarua, a port on Rarotonga's north shore, on March 21, 1915, and was buried in Mission Cemetery.

III

SAM BROWN
He Died With His Boots On

"Chief" is a term given to the top-notch gunslinger in a certain area. During the early 1860's Samuel Brown earned the title of "Chief" by becoming Utah Territory's most feared killer and gang leader. The Brown Band robbed stages, rustled cattle and had their hands into practically every illegal activity.

In the year 1860 alone, Sam knifed sixteen men before taking their money. Yet Brown and his men always stayed far out of the reach of the law, and never camped long in any one area. Another reason for their success was that nobody would testify against them, since witnesses knew it meant an early grave.

Whenever one of Brown's men was taken into custody, the local Sheriff was payed a visit by Samuel, whose guns spoke louder than words.

So unafraid was Brown that he would strut around saloons bragging about his killings. He had nothing to worry about, because no Marshal dared tangle with the fastest gun in Nevada.

Not only was he feared by white men, but by Indians as well. Brown and his men sacked Piute villages, scalped the tribesmen, and raped the squaws.

A week before Sam's thirtieth birthday, one of his men was jailed in Genoa for killing an innocent man who happened to have held the winning hand in a poker game. The badman was arrested and taken before Judge Cradlebaugh for a preliminary hearing. At this time a lawyer named Bill Stewart, acting on behalf of the prosecution, swore he would get the outlaw hanged.

This promise reached the ears of Sam Brown, who was already on the trail heading for Genoa. Once at the courthouse, Sam, who was decked out in his fighting gear, walked proudly down the aisle, interrupting a witness' testimony and sending all persons scrambling out the

22

windows and exits in a hurry. All persons that is, except for Bill Stewart.

Drawing a revolver, Stewart ordered Brown to the witness stand whereupon the Judge came back into the room. Stewart made Sam testify that the defendant had a bad reputation. Before long Brown had almost hanged his own man.

In an effort not to lose his stature as "Chief," Sam explained to the court that he had merely dropped by to retain Bill Stewart as his lawyer in a Plumas County murder case. Brown even gave Stewart a $500 retainer to prove his statement.

The jury, which had cautiously crept back to their seats, listened to Sam before finding the defendant guilty of murder. Brown's fellow outlaw was sentenced to be hanged.

Sam was so upset with himself, with Bill Stewart and with the jury, that he swore he would kill a man before going to bed that night. Since the objects of his hatred were out of reach, Sam chose an innkeeper to be his victim. Henry Van Sickles proved the wrong man to chose. Before Sam could explain what he was going to do, Henry emptied both barrels of his shotgun into the desperado's chest.

A coroner's jury found Henry not guilty, and further declared that Samuel Brown's predicament ". . . served him right." Utah Territory's notorious "Chief" was no more.

IV

MORGAN COURTNEY
Brain Rather Than Bronze Filled His Pockets

What happens when two miners, digging their claim, locate a rich vein of ore that goes into their neighbor's property? Tom and Frank Newlands found themselves in such a predicament in Southeastern Nevada's Lincoln County.

The time was 1870, and Jack H. Ely and W. H. Raymond were the Newlands' rich neighbors. Upon thinking over the situation, the Newlands decided to take the Ely-Raymond Mine by force. The brothers bought the talents of local toughs who served as guards while the Newlands continued digging their now unlawful claim.

Not to be outdone, Ely sent for Nevada's feared gunslinger, Morgan Courtney, who was "living it up" in San Francisco. Dressed in frilly clothes and a top hat, Courtney and three comrades, Michael Casey, Bernard Flood, and William Bethards, arrived in Lincoln County eager to do business.

Ely promised Courtney that if the gunfighter could get rid of the Newlands, he and Raymond would let him mine their rich claim for one month. Courtney sized up the problem, and he saw that he and his men were far outnumbered for a direct confrontation.

So he had one of his men deliver a large shipment of whiskey to the mine as if it were a gift from the Newlands' father who lived in Reno.

There was a gala time throughout the Newland Diggings as miners and guards "wet their whistles" late into the night. Meanwhile Courtney and his men waited in patience until shortly after midnight, when all sounds ceased as the merrymakers sprawled out on the ground.

Then, and only then, did the Courtney group attack the fortified mine. They met no resistance. Courtney placed the bad hombres in a wagon and sent it across the county line, warning them that they would be shot on sight.

The delighted miners, Ely and Raymond, lived up to their end of the bargain; and the Courtney gang got to mine the claim for thirty days. Directing his men, who did all the digging, Courtney earned close to $100,000 from the mine before leaving for San Francisco.

Unfortunately he did not stick to using his brains, and Morgan Courtney was gunned down years later in Pioche.

V

A. JACK DAVIS
He Pioneered Train Robbery in the West

Like Adolph Sutro, A. Jack Davis was a very respectable Virginia City businessman in the 1860's. He owned a mill in the Six Mile Canyon, and also served as the recorder for the Flowery District.

Jack Davis liked living in luxury, and to live in his style required more income than he made honestly. So Davis turned to robbing stages to bolster his finances. His mill served as both a blind for robberies, and as a place to rework stolen bullion.

Jack's favorite place to waylay coaches was along the Geiger Grade on the Reno-Virginia City stage run. Together with his gang of five well-chosen veteran bandits, he successfully looted six Wells Fargo shipments.

It was during one heist that Davis proved to be a gentleman road agent. After discovering two females aboard a stage he was in the process of robbing, Jack quickly provided coach cushions and blankets for the women, and even poured them champagne which he found in the cargo.

Part of the Davis gang's success in the stage banditry occupation came from a unique signal system Jack worked out. Davis would send two of his men to a distant mountain peak, and there they would ignite bondfires to indicate the number of guards on the stage.

But like all criminals Jack was eventually tracked down and thrown in the Virginia City jail. He was, however, freed after bribing the jury prior to his 1867 trial.

Once back in operation, Jack and his men turned to train robbery and carefully planned what would become the first train robbery in the Far West. It took place on November 4, 1870 as the Central Pacific Train Number One stopped at Verdi, eleven miles outside of Reno in the canyon of the Truckee River.

Two of Jack's men jumped aboard the cab, forcing the train to stop. The cars were unhitched, and Engineer

Small was ordered to take the locomotive and express car up the track several miles.

There the bandits broke into the strongboxes and made off with $42,000 in gold money. Not a shot was fired; and Wells Fargo Agent James B. Hume thought it to be a highly professional operation. Even the telegraph wires had been cut.

Sheriff James Kincaid of Washoe County rounded up a posse and went after the train robbers. Rewards were offered by the United States Post Office ($500), Wells Fargo Bank ($10,000), and the state of Nevada ($20,000).

Bounty hunters, posses, and local citizenry searched for clues. Finally a tavern keeper, Nick Pearson, of Sardine Valley, served three horsemen who stopped at his bar, then notified the Sheriff. By the end of the week the Jack Davis gang was behind bars.

Other members of the gang were John Squires, a veteran stage bandit; J. E. Chapman, Comstock gambler; E. B. Parsons, professional poker player; Tilton Cockerill, former army officer; and two men—Randy Roberts and George Gilchrist.

Jack admitted to being the ringleader of the train robbery, but he said he was forced into it because of the "unfair tactics used by Wells Fargo in adding extra guards to the stages."

On December 25, 1870 Jack Davis entered Nevada State Prison to begin a ten-year sentence. During the major prison break on September 17, 1871, Jack refused to escape and, instead he helped prison officials against his own peers. For this Davis won himself the Governor's pardon on February 16, 1875.

One would think Jack learned his lesson. Once out of jail, Jack regrouped his stage robbing gang and again began to hold up Concords. On the dark night of September 3, 1877 the mountaintop signal fires were placed too close together, and Davis thought there was only one messenger.

As he leaped out in front of the stage in White Pine

County, Jack was instantly killed by Wells Fargo guards Eugene Blair and Jimmy Brown. The stage went on to Tybo with its strongbox intact, thus bringing to an end the career of one of Nevada's most brilliant bandits.

VI

NEVADA'S RATTLESNAKE DICK
His Rattle Was Worse Than His Bite

Rattlesnake Dick was a California robber whose fame equaled that of such well-known bandits as Black Bart and Joaquin Murieta. But few students of the West know the story of the relatively unknown Rattlesnake Dick of Nevada.

The Nevada imposter's real name is unknown. Furthermore, nobody even knows why he stole the name of California's Rattlesnake Dick, unless perhaps he hoped it would lead him to a promising criminal career. It did not, however, because one just cannot compare a pistol to a cannon, and likewise one cannot compare the two Dicks.

Nevada's Rattlesnake never did make the big time. He was always thrown into jail for drunkeness, petty thievery, disturbing the peace, or "conning" someone out of their money. Reference to Dick is first made in a Nevada newspaper on May 16, 1863, the day he rode on the Austin Stage and "conned" a young lady out of her watch and money.

Once in Austin, Rattlesnake sold the watch and went on a drunken spree which led to Dick's purchasing the favors of one Bertha. After escorting Bertha up to her crib above the saloon, the con artist consumed so much liquor that he fell unconscious against the prostitute's door.

Because the "dead weight" was interfering with her business, Bertha had Dick dragged off and thrown in the street whereupon the Sheriff arrested him for obstructing traffic. Upon being released the next morning, Rattlesnake stomped back to the bar—"hell bent for leather 'n lead." Grabbing a club, which was propped up against the door, Dick came up behind the bartender, who was partially responsible for his arrest (for throwing Dick into the street) and let swing. The saloon employee was knocked senseless. Rattlesnake then rushed upstairs to even the score with Bertha.

Not finding her in he decided to wait, and while doing

29

so consumed much of the harlot's stock of booze. It was Miss Bertha who discovered the unconscious Rattlesnake, and he awoke in the pokey for the second time that day. Dick was released after the bartender admitted being hit from behind, never catching a glimpse of his attacker.

No sooner a free man then Rattlesnake stormed up to Bertha's crib once again. This time she was in, but she threw her charm on the angry bum and then for some unknown reason accepted his proposal of marriage.

A week later the two exchanged vows. Following the ceremony, a reception was held at a saloon near the chapel; and Rattlesnake got "pie-eyed" and fell to the floor in front of his bride, who left the tavern in a huff.

This time Dick chose the wrong saloon to get drunk in, and when he awoke he found out he had just been "shang-hied" into Company D of the First Battalion, Nevada Territorial Volunteers, who just happened to be recruiting drunks for the Army.

Rather than being upset Dick was honored, so honored that he ran to his new home and told his wife. When she declared what an absolute idiotic imbecile he was, Dick beat her up badly.

Angered as she never was before, Bertha got a shotgun and when Rattlesnake opened the front door that evening she emptied both barrels into his chest. An understanding jury acquitted Rattlesnake Dick's widow, and she went back to her former occupation of providing comfort for wealthy, womenless, Nevada miners.

VII

JOHN DOE
His Robbery Was Caught On Film

On August 15, 1905 the passengers on the Fresno to Yosemite Stage were reminiscing about the glorious days forty years back when stage robberies were a common occurrance. They were sure glad not to have traveled on stage back then.

It took but a few moments for them to swallow their words when the coach was ordered to halt in a small clearing. In disbelief the passengers peered out of the window to see what had to be a character out of the comic opera.

The bandit stood with his rifle resting over his shoulder and a pistol in his hand. He wore an old felt hat, a ragged duster, and moth-eaten clothes. Was this some kind of a put on? It was not.

The outlaw next ordered the passengers out of the stage and commenced to take their valuables. He refused the whip's and two blacksmiths' money declaring, "I don't want workingmen's money." Before thanking his victims and disappearing into the underbrush, the highwayman agreed to pose for a photo taken by one of the not-so-timid passengers.

Anton Veith, Austrian Consul to the United States and one of the victims, took what probably was the only known picture of an actual stage robbery. In an interview with the *Fresno Morning Republican*, Veith explains this peculiar episode.

"The bandit was a thorough gentleman. I can't imagine a man being more considerate of the people he was robbing. In some ways he was very clever, in other ways very careless. There was half a dozen times I might have shot him if I had a pistol and he didn't try to find out if any of the men had one or not. No one did.

"It was my first experience in a hold up and it was certainly worth $40. I don't know of any other case in which a photograph has been taken of a criminal at the time of the commission of the crime. The whole affair—our talking over the possibility of a robbery, then the surprise of it really happening and being taken by such a courteous robber—makes it a memory worth having."

A vigorous search by Sheriff Barnett failed to turn up a clue, but the Sheriff's personal belief was that the culprit was the "no-good" son of a bartender who lived at Coarse Gold Station. Sheriff Barnett told the barkeep's son his thoughts, and said that he would keep an eye on him. He was not bothered again by John Doe.

For more than half a century, this valuables box was what western highwaymen were after.

Courtesy of the Wells Fargo History Room.

John Allen, alias Sheet-Iron Jack, had a lot of close shaves in his career as a barber-bandit.

Courtesy of the Wells Fargo History Room.

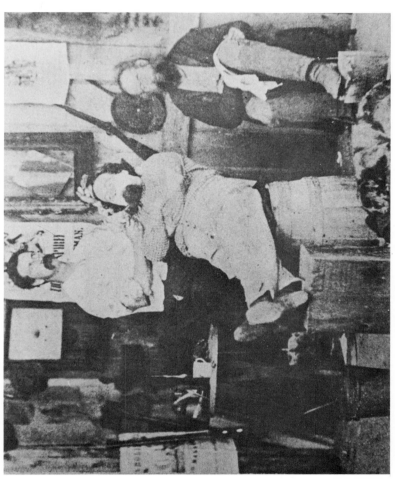

John Allen's barber shop in Shasta, California, looked like this in the 1860's. Courtesy of the Southern Pacific Company, San Francisco.

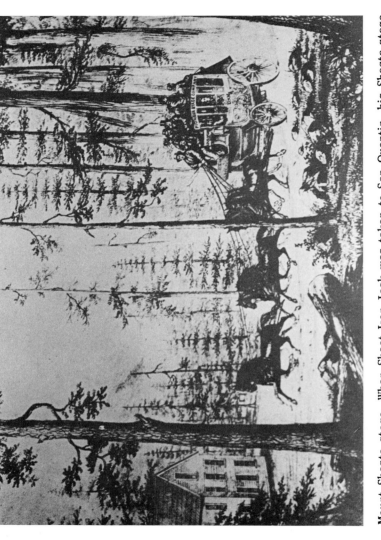

Mount Shasta stage. When Sheet–Iron Jack was taken to San Quentin, his Shasta stage was held up.

Courtesy of the Society of California Pioneers, San Francisco.

Charles Wells Banks, trusted Wells Fargo employee, shocked everyone when he vanished with over $100,000 in 1886.

Jack Davis and his gang carried out the first train robbery in the Far West on Novermber 4, 1870 near Verdi, Nevada. Courtesy of the Wells Fargo History Room.

Austin, Nevada was the home of the sagebrush menace, Rattlesnake Dick.
Courtesy of the Bancroft Library

On August 15, 1905, the only known photograph of an actual stage robbery in progress was recorded in Yosemite.   Courtesy of Yosemite National Park.

VIII

CHARLES H. DORSEY
*California's Complete Criminal
Sought and Got Excitement*

Charles H. Dorsey had everything going for him in Union City, Indiana during the 1850's. He was a prosperous merchant, a happily married man, and a deacon in his church. Neighbors used to take their problems—big and small—to Charles, who patiently listened to them before coming up with a sensible solution. There was even some talk of having Dorsey run for public office, but Charles did not like party politics.

From the outside, Charles Dorsey was thought by many acquaintances to be the perfect man—a model for small boys as well as husbands. But deep inside, Charles wanted something more: he dreamed of living an exciting, eventful life.

So when thousands of men left his native state of Indiana to head for California's gold-rich Mother Lode, Dorsey naturally followed suit. He left his loving wife and daughter in charge of the store, packed his goods, and headed for the Atlantic Coast.

He joined the Mutual Protection Trading and Mining Company, which consisted of sixty men who purchased the *Barque Emma Isidora*, a sailing vessel, to take them to San Francisco.

It was November of 1854 when the vessel reached San Francisco. Charles and all members in his Company had visions of working a few months, making a fortune, then returning to the East.

Once in San Francisco his group boarded a steamboat which took them to Sacramento. The honorable Charles Dorsey unfortunately became a suspect when a woman who he had been seen with was found stabbed to death aboard ship. Although he was innocent and acquitted of all criminal implications, the Mining Company voted to expel Charles, and when they reached Sacramento he was on his own.

33

Not one to let anything get the best of him, Charles boarded a stage for Volcano. Upon reaching Volcano he saw thousands of miners eagerly bustling around along Mokelumne River. Some were panning gold, some were shoveling dirt into long toms, and others were pumping water from holes with buckets. The men were dressed in ragged clothes and beatled around as if their lives depended on it. This looked like the type of excitement Charles Dorsey had dreamed about.

After a month of trying his luck at panning, then mining, Charles discovered that finding gold was not as easy as he had heard.

Gradually his values, morals and hopes left him, due to the combination of a severe winter, lack of correspondence with his family, hard luck as a miner, and the sins in which nearly all the prospectors around him participated.

Taking to the bottle, the once-respectable Union City merchant found himself "sleeping it off" in the Volcano jail. It was in the pokey that Dorsey came in contact with petty thieves as well as cold-blooded killers.

Two bandits persuaded the desperate miner to join them in a series of Wells Fargo stage robberies. Dorsey learned his new profession well, and soon became one of the gang's leaders. In the midst of his success, Charles was tracked down by famed Wells Fargo Detective James B. Hume, and he had a chance to think about where he went wrong while serving two terms in the penitentiary.

Unfortunately for him, while in San Quentin he came into contact with murderers and bank robbers, who taught the attentive Dorsey many of their tricks.

Following his release from prison, Charles went to Eureka where strangely enough, he got the idea to go "respectable" for awhile. The still handsome ex-bandit married another woman and settled down once again, managing a store.

Dorsey was accepted by the Eureka community and gained a reputation as a respectable, distinguished-looking gentleman. His business prospered, and one might think he had decided to go straight permanently.

For a couple of years he was content with living a dormant, uneventful life, much as before. Deep inside, however, Charles still had an urge for excitement, and when he accidentally met up with a fellow ex-con, the two decided to make a comeback in crime.

With his new partner, Paul Patterson, Dorsey ambushed the Eureka stage as it climbed a steep hill on September 1, 1879.

The stagewhip threw down the strongbox and the bandits ordered the passengers out on the road. When Patterson went around collecting the loot, one rider, William Cummings, leaped at the bandit and was coldly "cut down" by Dorsey. Cummings, a banker from Moore's Flat, gave his life in an attempt to save his valise which contained $7,000 in cash.

Quickly gathering the rest of the valuables, the two outlaws made a hasty get away into the underbrush. Unknown to Dorsey, one of the stage passengers had been his neighbor in Eureka. The Sheriff was notified of this fact, and Charles' description was circulated around Northern California. It was only a week before San Francisco Detective I. W. Lees, spotted Dorsey and made the arrest. Patterson was found nearby.

At the trial Patterson was sentenced to hang, but Dorsey was given a life imprisonment sentence. It seems that Charles was one of Quantrill's men, and a member of the jury thought of Quantrill as his idol. Thus he threatened to have a hung jury if the death penalty was given to Dorsey.

Charles Dorsey was hauled off to San Quentin to serve his sentence. At "Q" he made the acquaintance of George Shinn, alias Joe Thompson, who was a trustee and had gained the confidence of the prison officials. Together they worked up an escape plan.

Their plan centered around Shinn's job, for which he daily drove a cart outside the penitentiary walls. Taking advantage of a dark, rainy afternoon, Shinn drove to a distant corner of the field outside of San Quentin. Beneath a tarpaulin in his cart lay Charles Dorsey. They both sneaked off, stole a rowboat, crossed San Pablo Bay to Contra Costa, then headed toward Chicago where Shinn had friends.

They could not resist staying away from "The Golden State" for long, and two months later the desperadoes came back to California and held up three Wells Fargo stages. They took their loot to a hideout near Perkins on the American River.

Tired of "laying low," they decided to become involved in a different criminal activity—train robbery. Together they stopped trains outside of Pixley and Cape Horn Mills (Placer County). To stop the trains the outlaws put a buggy on the track, then forced their way into the baggage car.

The Cape Horn Mills train robbery took place on August 31, 1881 and netted them several thousand dollars. Following their successful holdups, Dorsey and Shinn returned to Chicago to wine and dine the women and to allow time for the posses to lose their trail.

The posses lost track of the two bandits, but Wells Fargo Agent James Hume did not. He was notified by an informant that two men, answering Dorsey's and Shinn's descriptions, were living in Chicago. Hume had to enlist the aid of Pinkerton men since he was known to the bandits, having put them away before. The Pinkerton men had no trouble locating Dorsey and Shinn in Chicago; and the two outlaws gave up without a fight.

The two desperadoes were taken before the magistrate and sentenced to a lengthy stay in a California prison. As a security measure, Hume made sure George Shinn was placed in Folsom, far away from the scheming Charles Dorsey who was put in San Quentin. Neither of them ever took part in crime again.

Ironically, the happiest man to see Dorsey taken into custody was a prisoner named George Nelson. Nelson was Dorsey's look-alike, and had an identical voice, which sent the innocent man to prison in a case of mistaken identity.

36

After Dorsey and Shinn escaped San Quentin, Thomas Davis, the foreman of a spread in Southern California, was held up. Nelson, who was traveling in the vicinity at this time, was arrested and positively identified as the robber by Davis.

Nelson served one year of a ten-year term before the real Charles Dorsey was captured. Dorsey confessed that he robbed Davis, thus freeing Nelson from the penitentiary. Oddly enough, Nelson was a native of Indiana, a deacon in his church, and a store merchant.

All in all Charles H. Dorsey had quite an unusual criminal career. He proved his versatility by performing his roles as a murderer, stage robber, prison escapee, polygamist and train bandit. His occupations enabled him to be branded by historians as, "California's Complete Criminal."

Not much can be said for a man who sacrifices everything for a career of crime, except that Charles Dorsey sought Excitement and he got his fair share.

IX

LOUIS DREIBELBIS
He Unknowingly Robbed His Own Bride

There they stood, Louis Dreibelbis and Miss Eleanor Berry, at the altar, about to become Mr. and Mrs. when low and behold, Eleanor got a good look at her fiance for the first time. She let out a shreak before racing out the back door. It seems Louis was the highwayman who had held up her stage moments before.

Eleanor was a mail order bride from Michigan, and she knew little about Louis. But she did want to come West, and this seemed the best way to do it.

Meanwhile Louis was plaguing the Colfax to Grass Valley Stage for many months and July 23, 1873 was a day of no exception. Using his shotgun he halted the Concord as it approached a steep hill outside of Grass Valley. Besides Miss Berry, United States Senator Sargent and Brigadier Charles C. Cadwalader were amongst the notables riding as passengers in the ambushed stage.

Stagewhip Bob Scott said that the next Concord carried the strongbox, but Louis located the loot inside cushions forming the rear seat of the coach. Having a horrible time opening the box, Louis started to light a piece of dynamite, when Miss Berry—neither of the two had seen each other prior—cried out, "My trousseau is in the trunk. Won't you take it down before the explosion?" Louis acknowledged the pretty school teacher's wish.

Dreibelbis netted $7,000 from the box before vanishing into the underbrush on horseback. The stage proceeded on to Grass Valley; and Miss Berry went to the predetermined chapel to meet her man. Bashful Louis met her in the dark church, and together they strolled down the aisle.

When they reached the candle-lit altar, Miss Berry, recognizing her fiance, decided to remain a Miss and vamoosed, but not before telling the Sheriff.

Wells Fargo Detective James B. Hume was dispatched to the scene in hopes of solving the series of Wells Fargo robberies in the Grass Valley area. At the top of his investigative list was Louis, who was calling himself Robert Walker.

Walker told Hume that he was the ex-superintendent of a Grass Valley mine, and the St. Patrick Mine at Ophir. Hume's telegrams proved Walker's words to be false; and after a few hours of questioning Louis admitted his part in the robberies.

The bandit told Hume that his accomplices were James Meyers, a Grass Valley saloonkeeper, and Nat Stover, a miner. For turning state's evidence and returning the stolen money, Louis Dreibelbis was set free and he went back to his home in Galena, Illinois where he claimed to have been Sheriff. Whether he ever got "hitched" is anyone's guess.

X

JAMES DUNHAM
Mass Murder Was His Contribution to Campbell

One of the gravestones in San Jose's Oak Hill Cemetery reads, "Vengeance is mine, I will repay, Saith the Lord." Beneath lie the victims of one of the most brutal multiple murders in Santa Clara County history.

James Dunham married the prestigious Colonel R. P. McGlincy's daughter Hattie in Campbell, California. It was an impressive society wedding; and all was champagne and roses for the first few months.

Gradually and for unknown reasons, the honeymoon faded away. It was known, however, that Dunham periodically broke out in temper tantrums. In 1896 a young son was born, but this joyful event unfortunately did not pull the family back together. The Dunhams were separated; and it was rumored that the Mrs. threw the Mr. out of the house.

On the dark night of May 26, 1896 James returned to his old home unannounced and quietly removed his shoes. His wife, mother-in-law, infant son, and servant were the only ones in the house at the time, and they had all retired for the evening. Without being seen, Dunham carefully gathered up several photos of himself and destroyed them.

Then in a scene out of a horror movie, James grabbed an ax and went on his mission of death. From one room to another he brutally murdered, first his wife, then the poor servant girl, and finally his mother-in-law. He let his baby son live, probably so that his child could inherit the McGlincy wealth.

Impatiently Dunham waited for over an hour in the dark farmhouse for the return of Colonel McGlincy, the Colonel's stepson, and a hired hand who were attending a religious meeting in Campbell.

When they arrived, James shot them without explanation before fleeing in an easterly direction on horseback. Somehow, one of the farmhands had escaped being a victim by hiding in the hayloft and hearing the nightmare.

Descriptions were posted throughout the Bay Area warning people to be on the lookout for a man "32 years of age, 6 feet, 160 pounds, dark hair, moustache, blue eyes, medium complexion, last seen wearing black suit, cutaway coat, black soft hat, number 9 shoes, sharp pointed toes and is an expert bicyclist." Dunham was also said to walk very erectly and to possess a chin which receded when he laughed.

James was last seen on the Mount Hamilton Road in the vicinity of the Smith Creek Hotel. He was never heard from again. James Dunham disappeared with the still-unknown motive for the brutal murders he left behind in Campbell's first and worst multiple murder.

XI

GORDON ELLIS
He Crippled Many Men

Back in the 19th Century there were several men who hobbled about on crutches in Nevada's Pahrump Valley.

Some of these chaps were victims of mining accidents, others were crippled by disease. But many of these men received their handicap from a ruthless, cold-blooded gambler named Gordon Ellis.

It was rumored that Ellis had been a one-time deputy sheriff in Placer County, California, but he was forced to flee after some prisoners failed to reach jail and were found shot to death by a group of law-abiding citizens.

Ellis drifted into Death Valley where he went into cahouts with L. Edward Thomas, a borax miner. For a couple of years the two men worked hard and their claim became quite valuable. Ellis, however, became tired of honest work and one day, without provocation, he "wasted" his partner with a shotgun blast, sold the mine, and moved on to Pahrump Valley—which was noted for its good time saloons, complete with gambling, girls, gangrene juice, and good grub.

The former miner was not one to take any lip; and when a Mexican gambler inferred that Ellis might be cheating, the accuser was shot in the right leg.

Ellis, who had been drinking, took a second aim for the Mexican's heart, but when he saw the gambler hobbling in agony for safety, he made a vow to continue to shoot people who got in his way in the right leg.

Gradually, more and more men were using crutches in the wild Pahrump Valley; and miners gave Ellis a wide berth.

But one night Ellis handicapped the wrong man. He was playing poker as usual when an Irishman, named Pat Shea, accused Ellis of pulling a card from his sleeve. Upon hearing Shea make his charge, the other card players scattered as if lightning had hit their table.

Calmly, Ellis stood up, drew his .45 and shot Shea

through the right leg. However, Shea was a tough Irishman, and he kept verbally abusing Ellis, who quickly lost his temper and went into a rage.

Ellis shot Shea in the left leg, then ordered the floored Irishman to stand up and fight. Much to Ellis' horror, the seriously-injured Shea got to his feet and painfully made his way toward Ellis, who got cold feet and ran out the door.

Somehow Shea managed to follow him. As Shea came through the swinging saloon doors, Ellis had regained his cool, and after taking careful aim, he shot the Irishman in the stomach.

Still Shea did not fall to the ground. Instead, he drew his own gun and placed one bullet through the heart of Ellis, who reportedly "died with a look of utter disbelief on his face."

Shea miraculously recovered from his wounds, and from that time on was known as the "curer of the handicapped" in Pahrump Valley.

XII

MANUEL GONZALES
He Had A $60,000 Secret

It was the Fall of 1885 in Ormsby County, Nevada, and a Wells Fargo Stage, carrying 300 pounds of bullion worth $60,000, was heading for the United States Mint at Carson City. It never reached its destination.

Manual Gonzales and his three partners halted the stage as it slowed down for a sharp bend in the road just outside of Carson City. The Highwaymen got away with the bullion plus $1,000 "contributed" by the stage's passengers.

The bandits galloped off to the Cook Ranch, ten miles West of the holdup site, where they had fresh horses waiting; but a fast moving posse caught up with them near the Pinenut Range and a gunfight ensued.

One road agent was killed, two escaped wounded on horseback (they were later found dead), and ringleader Manuel Gonzales was captured alive. The stolen bullion was not found.

Gonzales was sentenced to ten years in Nevada State Prison. Near the end of his term he got tuberculosis and nearly died. Wells Fargo executives, still hopeful of recovering the bullion, persuaded the Governor to pardon the bandit in hopes that Manuel would lead authorities to the loot.

Instead of going to the buried money, Gonzales went into Carson City where he was taken into the home of an old friend, George Hank, and even given a job in Hank's store. For over a year Manuel's health steadily improved, and he never rode out of Carson City. Then, one cold, snow flurry December day Gonzales told Hank about the robbery and agreed to take him to the hidden loot. As Gonzales mounted his horse he suffered a stroke and "cashed in his chips." To this day the bullion has not been unearthed, and is rumored to be either near the Carson City airport or within the shadow of Nevada State Prison.

XIII

J. P. HARMAN
He Drank From Rags To Riches To Rags

Two masked outlaws fired rifles into the late afternoon air as Southern Pacific's Oregon Express slowed down for a curve at Sheep Camp Crossing near Sacramento. It was October, 1894, and the "iron horse," hissing and screeching, came to a stop along the tule marshes of Yolo County.

Threatened with dynamite, a train guard opened up the express car. The captive crew was ordered to drag to the locomotive four Wells Fargo sacks containing $52,000 in ten-dollar and twenty-dollar gold pieces.

The engine was unhitched, and the bandits took off, plunging the locomotive into the darkness of the night. Moments later the bandits returned the unmanned train engine at full speed, causing it to crash into the stalled train, thus creating a wreckage that would hamper pursuit.

A few yards up the track the two robbers were dragging their loot to a predetermined hiding place near a tree in the marsh. Covering their loot with reeds, the laughing badmen mounted their horses and rode off toward Sacramento.

The joke was on them. Witnessing the entire incident was a blurry-eyed, red-faced tramp. Having fortified himself with liquid refreshment, this gentleman spent the evening propped against a tree near the tracks.

Knowing what he had just witnessed could never be true, a relaxed, carefree J. P. Harman fell fast asleep. The next morning, he awoke with a throbbing headache, thanks to the wine he had consumed and thanks too, to the vivid event of the night before. Had he really seen such a dramatic episode?

Staggering to his feet, J. P. waddled over to a nearby tree, where, much to his delight, he uncovered four sacks. He cut one open and gasped. Gold pieces spilled out before his eyes.

What could one do with such a discovery? No problem for J. P. He immediately reburied most of the money in tin cans at a location twenty yards further back in the marsh. The whistling hobo then "boarded" a freight train for San Francisco, never to be heard from—at least for awhile.

Two days later a gentleman faintly suggesting certain characteristics reminiscent of J. P. the tramp, turned up in the city. This handsome specimen certainly was no hobo but a baron, who, as he told the desk clerk in the Palace Hotel, had just arrived from Germany.

As a distinguished nobleman, Baron von Harmann was shocked to hear the gossip in San Francisco about the unsolved robbery of Southern Pacific's famed Oregon Express. Like any good businessman, however, he went to work—in a manner not unlike that of modern day tycoons.

The Baron moved into Fred Kordt's Saloon at 12 Oregon Street and made it his base of operations. He threw money around as if it were going out of style. But why not? After all, he told his acquaintances, he had "inherited" the money from an uncle in Germany.

First he gave Kordt $6,000 to fix up the saloon. Then $2,000 went for an interest in a racetrack. He gave George Riephof, a patent medicine merchant, thousands of green-backs which enabled him to sell a cure-all tonic in the streets of San Francisco. Finally there was the amply-endowed May de Vaughn, a princess in a local house of ill repute. She became the baron's mistress. So pleased was he that he built her an ornate, antique-filled pad at 625 Post St.

The Baron showed his appreciation in other ways too. He bought a railroad car and took May on a romantic journey across the United States. They stopped in the major cities along the way and stayed in the largest hotels, including New York's Waldorf.

When the lovers returned to San Francisco in January, 1896, they discovered someone had broken into their Post Street home. Oddly enough, the only thing missing was a diary with a damaging entry for October 12, 1894.

Meanwhile the robbers of the Oregon Express were

46

hunted down by authorities. One was killed, and the other, Jack Brady, told his whole discouraging tale to Wells Fargo detectives.

On February 2, a strange development occurred. While the Baron was quaffing his favorite ale in Kordt's Saloon, he was greeted with a tap on the shoulder. He turned to face detective John Thacker, who stood with badge in hand. The fairy tale only a drunk could believe had come to an end.

How had Thacker tracked down his man? He had located J. P. Harman, alias Baron von Harmann, through a Sacramento bum named Augustine. J. P. had made the mistake of sending Augustine to his "burial ground" when he needed more money. Fellow hoboes told Thacker about Augustine, who, in turn, told authorities about the baron. From this information, lawmen were able to locate $11,000 still buried.

At the Sacramento trial of J. P. Harman, Kordt, Riephof, and May "sang" when faced with prison sentences. But the one really left "holding the bag" was Wells Fargo Bank. Wells Fargo ended up with the mortgages on two saloons, the Post Street home, and a bank account worth $2,000 deposited under the name Baron von Harmann in the German National Bank.

Across the nation, newspapers made J. P. a national celebrity—"The last of the bigtime spenders," and the "man who singlehandedly made Wells Fargo Bank the nation's laughing stock."

It all came to an end when Judge Hinkson sentenced J. P. Harman to three years in Folsom Prison after the jury found him guilty of grand larceny. Did the Baron have any regrets? Well, his final words to the jury were, "I lived like a prince. The only thing I regret is that they didn't leave me alone long enough to spend it all."

After serving his time, J. P. waddled off toward the tule marshes near Sacramento, to be forgotten by all but Wells Fargo accountants. His fellow hoboes could never come close to the tales of their peer, Baron von Harmann, the tramp who lived two lives—both with style and grace.

XIV

JACK HARRIS
The Highwayman Who Became a Leading Detective

Many men got the urge to come to California during the Gold Rush, and Jack Harris of Massachusetts was no exception. He came to San Francisco via the Isthmus and decided to hunt gold in Marysville. Not finding the "elephant," Jack became a highwayman and took gold from those who had hit paydirt.

With the posse "hot on his trail" in California, Harris moved to Washoe—Carson City, to be exact. Here he bought a saloon and reportedly married the daughter of a successful Comstock miner in 1865.

Once settled down Jack took up his old job as road agent. On Friday nights, when he told his wife he was going to business meetings, Jack held up Pioneer Stages running between Virginia City and Placerville. For his efforts he was arrested, and although set free for lack of evidence, Jack lost his wife who moved back with her Virginia City parents.

Harris moved on to Austin and purchased a saloon which he ran for a couple of years before assuming a similar position in Hamilton. Things went well for Jack until he got in a duel with one of Hamilton's leading citizens and was forced to move to Pioche.

No sooner had he reached the "rip-roaring, blood and guts" city of Pioche, then Harris resumed his trade as a stage bandit. He was so good at waylaying Wells Fargo Concords that the stageline worked out a deal with him in which he received a monthly wage to sit out in front of the Wells Fargo office when the coach arrived. In this manner the stage company thought it would be impossible for Jack to hold up their stages.

Jack, however, was a clever bandit and he worked up a scheme to collect money both ways. With kerchief over his face, Harris would hold up the stage out on the trail, then race back to the Pioche station and sit in a chair to greet the stage when it arrived. Needless to say the contract was terminated and Jack eventually retired.

Possessing more money than he knew what to do with, Jack Harris moved on to Washington Territory. In the 1880's he became a police detective and compiled a remarkable record for apprehending the dishonest. Blessed with the knowledge that only a successful criminal can have, Harris proved an excellent tracker, almost always getting his man. Quite a surprising turn around for Nevada's clever outlaw, but then again, Jack Harris was always a surprising man.

XV

PEARL HART AND JOE BOOT
They Didn't Know How to Hide

The Benson-Globe Stage was winding its way across an Arizona road on the sweltering day of May 30, 1899, when it approached a man and boy on horseback. Had this been thirty years earlier, the stage driver would have reached for his shotgun, but stage robbing was a thing of the past—or so the driver and passengers thought.

But as the stage neared the men, the horse riders drew guns and told the driver to get his hands up. The passengers were then ordered out, and the young boy shook each passenger down, collecting $5 from the sleeve of a Chinaman, $20 from the driver's pocket, $378 from the billfold of a traveling salesman and $37 from the clothes of a young Easterner.

The robbery victims would later tell the sheriff that the boy bandit was about five-foot-two, fifteen years old, His trousers didn't fit; and many of the passengers thought the cool-eyed lad was the son of the highwayman.

Although the stage riders were accurate in much of their description, the young outlaw was no one's son. In fact, "he" was a married female—the mother of two small daughters who were at their grandparents' home in Toledo, Ohio.

A month before the robbery, Mrs. Pearl Hart and her husband, Norman, had been cooks in a Mammouth mining camp in Arizona. However, Norm had run off with a popular lady of the night, causing Pearl to send her children home to her parents with the last amount of capital she possessed.

Adding to the problems, a letter was sent to Pearl informing her that her mother was critically ill. The lack of stage fare to Toledo played a large part in her teaming up with a down and out miner, Joe Boot, in the stage robbery scheme.

Both robbers were amateurs, yet they were able to pull off the $440 robbery with relative ease. However, escaping was the hard part; and they had not given any thought to how they were going to elude the posse.

Neither had any close friends in the area with whom they could hide. Not knowing where to go, Mrs. Hart and Mr. Boot did what common sense told them to do—travel in the opposite direction of the stage as fast as one can.

Mounting their horses, the road agents started down the stage road, then decided to leave it for the mountain wilderness. Their hastily-made escape plan was to stay in hiding during the day and travel at night.

In an effort to elude the posse they doubled back and forth over their trail while meandering through canyons and streams. So far they had been successful in their avoiding the posse, but criss-crossing confused them until they became helplessly lost.

Finally they rode into Cane Springs Canyon, and much to their horror they found themselves back at the scene of the robbery.

In a frantic panic the two highwaymen galloped off as fast as their horses would carry them until they came to Riverside, where they spotted a group of men, who later turned out to be miners, heading in their direction.

In a frenzy the robbers rode into the wilderness until they reached a large thicket of trees, where they camped for the night.

The thicket was not far from the railroad tracks, and they evidently considered leaving the area on a train. But the first freight which passed them had five armed guards sitting on a flat car, and the outlaws rode off—crossing their trails—until they unexpectantly happened on their old town of Mammouth.

They foolishly risked getting captured by returning to Joe's cabin for food and smokes. Exhausted, they spent the night in the cabin before heading for an abandoned mine just before dawn.

Perplexed by the difficulties of their new profession, the odd couple wasted half a day sitting in the cool mine before moving to an empty cave a couple of miles up the road.

With nightfall approaching, the couple became hungry;

51

and Joe went out in search of food. He located a wild hog, shot it, and spent the rest of the night wrestling it back to the makeshift hideout. They tried cooking it in the cave, but the acrid smoke forced them to barbeque the hog outside.

Once again before dawn, the dynamic twosome moved out—this time to an old schoolhouse on the outskirts of Mammouth. After feeding hay to the horses and hog's meat to themselves, Pearl and Joe proceeded to nap once again in some bushes outside of the schoolyard.

The shrill sound of an approaching train gave Joe an idea. Why couldn't he jump from a nearby hill onto the locomotive top, overpower the engineer, and stop the train so that Pearl could get on before making their escape by rail?

Pearl thought it a great idea, especially since this freight didn't seem to have any guards on it. Pearl anxiously waited several hundred yards up the track, as Joe prepared to hijack the freight.

But as the freight approached, Joe jumped on the locomotive and his forward momentum carried him off the roof crashing into the opposite hillside. Pearl watched with wonder as the train passed her and disappeared out of site.

She finally noticed Joe sitting dazed by the track. They rested once again, waiting for nighttime. That night they rode to a Mexican village about ten miles south of Mammouth, where Joe said he had a friend. But once again they spotted a group of men on the road, whom they mistook for posse; and the outlaws quickly left the road.

So quickly in fact that Joe's horse almost drowned in an irrigation ditch. His horse became so lame that the two robbers had to bed down until morning. To compound things, a storm hit the village, awakening the outlaws, who decided to move on.

The rain had left a good set of tracks for the determined posse to follow; and later that evening when they went to sleep, Pearl and Joe were rudely awakened by men's voices.

For Mrs. Hart and Mr. Boot getting captured was a real relief, because they were getting downright discouraged with their prospects for escape. All of the stolen money was recovered and returned to the robbery victims.

Joe and Pearl received ten year prison terms in Yuma Territorial Prison. However, after serving two and one-half years, Pearl was paroled for being a model prisoner. The Yuma prison was not built to accommodate female prisoners; and it is said the warden was glad to parole Pearl, who for six months afterward traveled around the country performing in the play, "The Arizona Bandit," before going to her mother's home in Toledo where she forever disappeared from newsprint.

XVI

DOMINGO HERNANDEZ
A Stack of Ears Adorned His Saddle

People never asked Domingo Hernandez about the stack of ears decorating his saddlebow, for if they dared their ears would undoubtedly be added to the collection. Each ear stood for a victim who met his death at the hands of the coldblooded and ruthless killer, who loved to see his fellow man die in pain.

While a sargeant in the Spanish forces, Hernandez deserted his troops in 1846, near Natividad, to start his psychopathic life of butchery. Nobody knows why Hernandez turned bad; but it is known that his motto was, "Dead men tell no tales."

Hernandez followed the same *modus operandi* in each incident. He would stop a lone traveler in the middle of a trail during the hours of darkness, asking the man for a match so that he could light his cigar. Domingo said, "Thank you," and as the stranger rode away he would be shot in the back.

He then robbed the victim, cut off one of his ears, and pushed the body down the deep ravines of La Cuesta de los Pinacates.

Domingo had ten ears in his collection before justice caught up with him. A sheriff's posse located the killer who cowardly gave up without a fight. He was taken to Monterey, where in 1846, Judge Florencio Serrano sentenced the murderer to be hanged.

Of all things luck came to the killer, for as he was being hanged the rope broke loose and he jumped to the ground; and a chase began which took authorities throughout Monterey. Finally Domingo was located in a stable where he once again surrendered meekly. However, on his trip back to jail, a group of Hernandez' outlaw peers shot two deputy sheriffs, allowing Domingo to vanish in the darkness of the night.

The psycopath resumed his old trade and began "knocking off" lone travelers on the Soledad Road. Soon he was caught by another posse in Santa Cruz (in 1849) and hanged by a good rope, thus ending his career. Domingo's own ears were chopped off and exhibited in Santa Cruz as a reminder to those who might have been considering starting a collection of ears.

XVII

TOM HORN
A Thorn in the Side of the Law

There are several examples of bad men who saw the light, turned over a new leaf, and in some cases became outstanding leaders of their communities and lawmen.

Tom Horn of Arizona was not such an example. In fact, he was just the opposite. The Missouri-born cowboy, who had been raised by Apaches, was a courageous, loyal Indian scout in the latter part of the nineteenth century.

Many historians give him the main credit for the capture of Indian chief Geronimo. It was Horn who endlessly trailed the old warrior and got the chief to agree to meet with General Nelson A. Miles.

Later, Horn served as a middle man in the Army-Indian peace talks. The six-foot-tall Spanish-American War veteran was also an excellent rodeo performer, and he later became the world champion steer roper.

Horn also had a distinguished career with the famed Pinkerton detective agency. While with Pinkerton he singlehandedly arrested a noted outlaw, Peg Leg McCoy. But Horn was a restless fellow, and he made it a practice not to stay long on any particular job.

Leaving Pinkerton, Horn became a bounty hunter. In his new capacity he enjoyed the company of cattle barons, who would often offer him additional bonuses for exterminating men who plagued them.

His reputation as one who got his man made him infamous throughout Arizona and Wyoming; and it is said that men took the long way around Horn in a saloon.

The qualities that made Horn a success in all of his professions included determination, loyalty to employer, and courage. While waiting to assassinate a cattle rustler, Horn patiently put up with snow storms and hunger pangs. His identifying mark was a rock under the victim's head. Cattle rustlers quickly got the message, and tried to avoid sections of the states where Horn had been seen.

Lawmen, many of whom had respected Horn in earlier days, tolerated him until an innocent man was murdered.

Willie Nickell, 14, the son of a sheep man, was ambushed by Horn one evening near a cattle baron's pasture. This proved to be the final straw; and Joe Lefois, a deputy U.S. Marshal was called in to track down Horn.

Oddly enough, the two men, who shared similar backgrounds became good friends; and one night during a drinking spell, the forty-two-year-old bounty hunter told Lefois about the Nickell ambush.

Lefois took the one-time Pinkerton detective to a local jail where he was locked up. Although he denied confessing to the killing of Nickell, Horn was found guilty by a jury, and the judge sentenced him to be hanged.

The cattle barons, who had not forgotten Horn's loyalty, devised an escape plan which called for the dynamiting of a jail wall. The plan was discovered by an alert deputy. In another jailbreak attempt, Horn and a fellow prisoner got as far as the town stable before being recaptured.

The state militia was called in, and on Nov. 20, 1903, the former lawman was hanged before a packed-street crowd. Much to the dismay of lawmen, Horn refused to identify his employers, even when he was asked a final time atop the gallows.

XVIII

LYDIA JOHNSON
The Confederates' Top Spy Was A Lady

Back in the 1860's when the Comstock Lode was bubbling with activity, a young lady was helping the Confederates in the Civil War by spying in Nevada. Petite Lydia Johnson was the gal whose past is shrouded in mystery.

Little is known about Lydia. She was thought to be a widow who had lots of money and lived in an attractive but small house in Virginia City. Lydia was a friend of the "Virginians," and she waved to them while making her mysterious daily ride across the mountains.

What is known for sure about Lydia is that she was a friend of nearly every mining official and stageline owner in the state.

It is suspected that she used her friendship to find out where gold and bullion shipments were being delivered and when. It was not long before large shipments of gold and silver started disappearing "lock, stock and barrel."

Tracks of the suspected highwaymen never turned up, but government officials believed that the loot was taken aboard a fast sailing vessel which went to the Isthmus. From there it was suspected to be transported to Mexico and on up to Texas where it reached the hands of the Confederates, who were in desperate need of capital.

Friends of Lydia Johnson were the ones being victimized in Nevada, but it was a long time before this mysterious woman was implicated in the scheme.

The Federal Government sent a secret group of soldiers to Virginia City to investigate the gold and silver disappearances. A Major Jeffers was leading the "hush-hush" investigation, but Jeffers could uncover nothing.

Then, somehow, Lydia Johnson's mysterious early morning rides got into the conversation, and Jeffers immediately got a warrant for her arrest—but Lydia was not to be found. Miss Johnson was evidently "tipped off" about the warrant and "hightailed it" out of the state.

The next mention of Lydia came in a miner's journal. James Henderson wrote on December 19, 1863, "Coming over the divide tonight [I] met Lydia Johnson riding toward Gold Hill, and riding much too fast for that dangerous road. Just on the edge of Virginia City [I] met three men, also riding fast. One was Major Jeffers. [I] didn't know the other two."

Nothing else was recorded about this episode until several years later, when Lydia Johnson's skeleton—and that of her horse—was found at the base of a mine shaft. It seems while Lydia was escaping Major Jeffers she took a wrong turn on the road at night and fell into the abandoned mine shaft.

The real truth as to who Lydia Johnson was will probably never be known unless turned up by a Civil War scholar in the archives of the Confederacy; but it can be stated that she served the Confederate cause like a true trooper, and died in the line of duty.

XIX

SIMONE JULES
This Mustachioed Gambler Died of a Broken Heart

In 1850 Simone Jules, a twenty-year-old French citizen, arrived in San Francisco on a Spanish ship. Before being in the city a week she got a most unusual job as a croupier for the roulette game in the Bella Union saloon.

A San Francisco newspaper editorialized that Simone should be barred from the saloon because "a woman's place is in the home." This publicity brought hundreds of curious patrons to the Bella Union to see the only female croupier in the city by the bay.

In 1853 Miss Jules decided to venture to Nevada City, California where she heard "men were in need of women." So she took her $8,000 out of the bank, boarded a stage, and set out to make her fortune.

On June 15 the dark-eyed beauty got off the stage and rented a room at the National Hotel. She created quite a stir with the male populous who had seen her get off the stage because she stayed in seclusion for nearly one week.

Then one morning Nevada citizens awoke to see "Madame Eleanore Dumont's Gaming Parlor" on Broad Street. Where Simone Jules came up with the name Eleanor Dumont is still uncertain, but it is believed that she picked up the name from a friend in San Francisco.

The miners flocked to her gaming establishment in hopes of playing a game of "vingt et un" or blackjack which Madame Dumont dealt herself. Miss Dumont's parlor was an overnight success—so much so that she needed to hire three other blackjack dealers. One of the new dealers was a handsome New York gambler named David Tobin. Tobin was in his early thirties, and the two hit it off quite well from first sight. It was not long until Madame Dumont gave Tobin a fourth of the proceeds. He proved his worth as a silent partner by organizing poker and faro games and putting in a large roulette wheel.

Most of the townspeople did not object to Miss Dumont's operation because she did not permit bad language or fighting in her parlor. She was even known to have grubstacked several down-and-out miners whose funds and luck had run out.

For over a year the parlor prospered. Then, for some unexplained reason, Tobin demanded more of the action. Madame Dumont refused and said she did not need a man to help her. In anger, she payed Tobin for his quarter interest in the operation. Dazed, David Tobin returned to New York, probably wishing he had not asked for more money.

Miss Dumont, who was really in love with Tobin and had some second thoughts about her actions, hoped that David would return. He never did, and Madame Dumont's life went rapidly downhill.

The miners started leaving for richer diggings; and within six months Simone Jules, alias Madame Eleanor Dumont, had lost her investment.

For five years she wandered from one camp to another trying to forget Tobin and her hard luck. In a Tri City gambling hall while dealing blackjack, Simone overheard a miner telling a friend, "I'll bet she was a real beauty when she was young."

This statement infuriated Simone who in her "age" sported a thin soft line along her upper lip—prompting miners to call her "Madame Mustache."

Simone lived up to the first part of her wicked nickname by getting together a bunch of young harlots and opening up "Madame Moustache's House of Pleasure" in San Francisco. According to legend one of her women was Martha Canary—a lady who later became known as Calamity Jane in dime novels.

While in San Francisco, Simone met an old female friend from Nevada City. From her Miss Jules learned that David Tobin had been seen in Carson City, Nevada.

Simone set out at once for Carson City, only to discover that the rumor proved false. Wanting to settle down, Simone married a man she had met in a saloon a week before. Daniel Carruthers, a retired Colonel in the Army, was the lucky man.

But Carruthers was a smooth talking opportunist, and before one month of marriage had ended he left one night with Simone's hard-earned cash. Outraged as she had never been before, Mrs. Carruthers took off after her husband, shotgun in hand. She caught up with him in a Carson City saloon and gunned him down. Madame Moustache quickly left town ahead of a mob, and headed for Bodie, California where the Lucky Boy strike was proving fruitful.

For a few weeks she once again dealt blackjack, and was well-liked by the miners for her easygoing personality and quick wit.

However, on September 7, 1879, Simone learned from a reliable former acquaintance in San Francisco that David Tobin had died thirteen years earlier in New York.

This news proved to be the final straw in Simone Jules' pitiful life. The next morning she was found dead in her cabin. An empty bottle of poison lay on the floor near her bed.

On September 9, 1879 The *Sacramento Union* gave a brief obituary on Simone Jules, who was known in the Mother Lode mining camps as Eleanor Dumont.

"BODIE Sep. 8—A woman named Eleanor Dumont was found dead today about a mile from town. She was well known throughout the mining camps."

There is no telling as to how Madame Moustache would have been remembered if David Tobin had returned to her side. Together they were successful, separated they died.

XX

JULIAN-SEXGIL-YOSCOLO
Horses Were Their Bag

Santa Clara County was the stomping grounds for the brother bandit-horse thief team of Yoscolo and Julian. They successfully robbed lone travelers of money and horses in the early 1840's. They maintained a large corral for stolen horses in the foothills of Mount Hamilton. The career of this motley duo came to an abrupt end one November day when a posse of angry Spaniards caught up with Yoscolo and beheaded him on the spot in 1843.

Yoscolo lost his head in the Santa Clara hills, but Julian miraculously escaped, heading for the area now known as Los Gatos. There he teamed up with Sexgil, one of California's finest horse thieves.

Somehow the Governor's messenger got hold of Julian and Sexgil and told them that they would be pardoned if they could catch the butchers who were killing government stock. After surveying the situation the two thieves decided to steal the government stock themselves. The Governor's own troops caught up with the two and sent them to Mexico, where they served out the rest of their days behind bars.

XXI

DUTCH KATE
Her Mouth Cost Her A Small Fortune

There were many characters in the old Far West of the 1850's, and not all of them were male. Dutch Kate was such an exception. Dressed in mens baggy clothes, Dutch was a familiar sight in the Marysville saloon. Western authority Captain William Banning said, "Kate could swear to do justice to any occasion." She also drank whiskey straight, chewed tobacco, smoked Havana cigars, and gambled with miners.

In fact few of her acquaintances ever truly believed she was a female. As was often the case in the West, gambling was the obsession which turned Dutch Kate into a stage-coach robber.

It all started on September 7, 1858 when Kate lost heavily in a poker game. Not only was her $2,000 life savings gone, but she became heavily in debt when she borrowed money. Marysville gamblers always saw to it that debtors made payments, one way or another, and Dutch Kate was not treated any differently.

Under the threat of being pistol-whipped if she did not "fork over" the money, Dutch agreed to make her payment in a lump sum the next morning.

Recruiting the help of two worthless brothers who could be trusted as far as one could throw them, Kate made plans to rob a stage. Before taking on the new assignment she and her gang stopped off at the Forest City Saloon to down a few drinks for the road.

Although Kate could usually hold her own, she had a bit too much liquid refreshment, which tended to loosen her tongue. The plans for the stage robbery slipped out, and an attentive bartender relayed them to a Wells Fargo stage-hand who put an empty strongbox on the Concord.

Dutch Kate's stick-up went almost like clockwork. One of the passengers, John H. Carmany, describes the action. "As we slowly ascended the grade with the heavy load,

Charles Dorsey made a complete turnabout by going from deacon to desperado.　　Courtesy of the Wells Fargo History Room.

FOR
CALIFORNIA!
Mutual Protection
Trading & Mining Co.

Having purchased the splendid, Coppered and very fast Sailing

Barque EMMA ISIDORA,

Will leave about the 15th of February. This vessel will be fitted in the very best manner and is one of the fastest sailing vessels that goes from this port.

Each member pays 300 dollars and is entitled to an equal proportion of all profits made by the company either at mining or trading, and holds an equal share of all the property belonging to the company. Experienced men well acquainted with the coast and climate are already engaged as officers of the Company. A rare chance is offered to any wishing a safe investment, good home and Large profits.

This Company is limited to 60 and any wishing to improve this opportunity must make immediate application.

An Experienced Physician will go with the company.

For Freight or Passage apply to 23 State Street, corner of Devonshire, where the list of

Gold hunter Charles Dorsey came to California on this ship, the *Isidora*, before embarking upon the criminal career that put him in San Quentin for life. Author's Collection.

Volcano Jail. It was in this pokey that Dorsey came into contact with hard-core criminals, who taught the greenhorn their trade.   Photo by Craig MacDonald.

The appearance of Drytown has changed little since the days when Dorsey's gang robbed stages in these foothills.

Photo by David Hillman.

Pioche, Nevada. Jack Harris was so successful at holding up Wells Fargo stages near Pioche, that the express lines paid him not to. Harris later became a leading detective in Washington.
Courtesy of the Nevada Historical Society.

In October 1894, train robbers halted the famed Oregon Express near Sacramento. Threatened with dynamite, the guard eventually opened the express car. Courtesy of the Wells Fargo History Room.

Silver City, Nevada. Lydia Johnson, mysterious Confederate spy, was seen as far south as Silver City in the late 1860's.

Courtesy of the Nevada Historical Society.

Jarbidge, Nevada. Anxious miners waited at Jarbidge for the stage on the payday of December 5, 1916. The stage never arrived. A posse learned that Ben Kuhl had killed the driver and stolen the money.

Courtesy of the Northeastern Nevada Museum.

Clement Lee's gang robbed stages at night and operated a popular Virginia City gambling parlor during the day.   Courtesy of the Nevada Historical Society.

It was faro and poker that led Hank Parrish to the gallows. This old photo shows faro players in Utah, where Hank learned the game.

Courtesy of the Utah Historical Society, Salt Lake City.

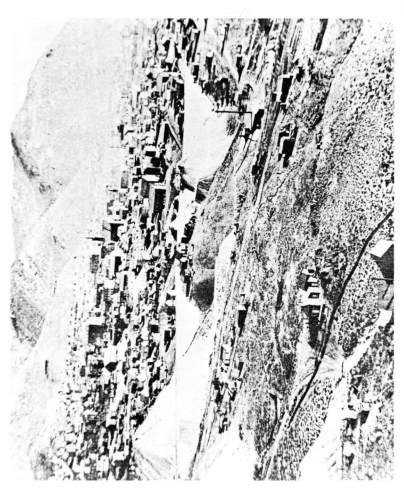

Virginia City, Nevada looked like this when Langford Peel was forced into becoming chief of the gunslingers.   Courtesy of the Nevada Historical Society.

Richard Perkins went from one of California's most notorious
outlaws to a prominent Kentucky politician.

Sheriff J. H. Adams of San Jose rounded up several Confederate Robin Hoods operating in California at the time of the Civil War.

It was all male juries like this one that usually let cattle rustler Susan Raper off the hook because of her charm and beauty.

Courtesy of the Idaho Historical Society, Boise.

The infamous Nick Rodriguez gang always met at Devil's Gate, Nevada, before a job.
Courtesy of the Nevada State Museum.

An early artist sketched this likeness of Nick Rodriguez, Nevada's Dr. Jedkyll-Mr. Hyde.

the horses were suddenly stopped without any demonstration, the express box ordered thrown down, followed by a wild scream from a scared woman . . ."

When Kate discovered the empty box she was disappointed to say the least. The obviously flustered bandits contemplated robbing the passengers, but decided not to. Carmany explains: "No doubt the bungling manner of the unsuccessful holdup was due to the late ticketing of the five gold-seeking tenderfeet, thereby overcrowding the stage to the great surprise and discomfort of the highwaymen."

Reluctantly, and with a thunder of profanity, she let the stage pass on through. Little did she know that a banker named Daniel Nichols was carrying a bag containing over $15,000 in gold.

Typical of so many western characters, Dutch Kate faded off into the sunset and was never seen or heard from again.

XXII

LIZZIE KEITH
This Sixteen-Year-Old Robbed Concords

Lizzie Keith was not like most beautiful sixteen-year-old girls in California in 1874. Instead of being married and a mother, the graciously-endowed lady took up a far more dangerous and unladylike profession: Liz was a stagecoach bandit.

Suffering from a broken home, Lizzie teamed up with a couple of male petty criminals to hold up stages between Hollister and Sonora. Her partners were bold with their plans; but when it came down to the "nitty-gritty" Lizzie was the only one not flustered.

It was a January morning when the bandits ordered the stage from Sonora to halt. Veteran whip, William Oliver (of the A. N. Foster Stage) brought his whip down on the heads of Lizzie's two accomplices—who ran away, but Liz did not. She just cocked back her shotgun like she meant business, and Oliver reluctantly gave up the rich New Idria Mine payrolls.

Most women stagerobbers would be content with such a "take," but Miss Keith was not. She waited until Oliver made the return trip with another payroll. This time Lizzie alone stood in the path of the Sonora stage, ordering it to halt.

Not to be victimized twice, Oliver sent his whip a-cracking on the girl's head, sending her face down in the dust. Both payrolls were recovered; and Lizzie Keith was transported to the Hollister jail, where she served a year sentence before being set free, never to return to crime again.

XXIII

BEN KUHL
His Bloody Shirt Done Him In

Treasure seekers probably know that $3,000 is buried somewhere in a canyon near Jarbidge, Nevada. The loot was hidden there by Ben Kuhl, one of Nevada's last great stage bandits. The time was December, 1916, Kuhl's final robbery was made possible because Jarbidge did not have the population to require a bank, so miners had merchants cash their paychecks. The merchants' money arrived by Concord.

The prospectors anxiously awaited the stage's arrival on the payday of December 5. Miners were eager to wash the dust from their thirsty throats and to buy the affections of a pretty face. But the stage did not arrive. A search by the Sheriff and his posse uncovered the coach, off the side of the road, partially hidden by willows.

Driver Frank Searcy was dead, with a bullet through the head, and the mail sack, $3,000 in cash, and a bag of coins valued at $200 were gone. The posse combed the surroundings and found a black overcoat, stained with blood, near the Jarbidge River. Nearby, a shirt with an "H" on it and a blue bandana kerchief were discovered.

The Sheriff identified the shirt as that belonging to Ben Kuhl, a miner whose cabin lay but a mile East of the shirt's location. The angry posse dragged the "innocent pleading" Kuhl out of his cabin; and though there was talk of lynching, Ben was taken to jail.

The bloody palm print on the mail bag was introduced as evidence against Ben during the trial at Elko on September 18, 1918.

As a last effort to save his life, Ben went before the Nevada Board of Pardons on December 13 to plead his guilt. It was then that Kuhl revealed that Stagewhip Frank Searcy had planned the whole robbery and was supposed to fake resistance during the robbery. The driver got cold feet at the last minute, according to Ben, so Kuhl killed him.

The Nevada Board of Pardons sentenced Kuhl to life imprisonment. Before dying, Ben Kuhl spent one of Nevada's longest terms behind bars—a total of twenty-seven years.

XXIV

CLEMENT LEE
He Borrowed the Wrong Overcoat

In the early 1860's Virginia City, Nevada hosted some of the biggest gaming establishments in the Far West. The rich Comstock Mines produced the capital necessary to insure the subsistence of the luxuriously furnished houses of luck. One such house was owned and operated by Clement Lee and his three associates.

Laughing miners with "pokes" of gold dust and greenbacks would rush feverously to the gaming tables where Lee was only too happy to relieve them of their burdens. But Clement was not satisfied with his gains—he sought and dreamed for much more.

He wanted to run the biggest gaming palace in Virginia City, and to do so would require thousands of dollars more than he had. So Lee and his associates took up the art of stage robbing. What made them unique among highwaymen was their unusual *modus operandi*.

Every Saturday night at midnight they would close down the gaming tables in their combination saloon-gambling hall. For the next few minutes they made sure they were seen throughout the building before sneaking out a back door, where horses stood awaiting their nights task.

The four mysterious men rode at a gallop through the dangerous, boulder-laden Dead Man's Gulch. Once beyond the Gulch they picked up fresh horses, stashed in the underbrush, and rode onward toward Reno. Then they branched off to the route which led to Honey Lake.

It was on this path that they held up the Reno Stage. The Lee Gang had a remarkable record of success, and soon they would have enough money to open their long-desired gambling palace. A couple more jobs and they could retire from the outlaw business forever.

One July moonlit night the four desperadoes approached the Concord as usual, but the driver did not see them until it was too late. The stage wheels grazed Clement's overcoat, producing a horizontal brown dirt mark on it.

69

Shots were exchanged between a deputy sheriff riding on the coach and Lee's band. The stage finally stopped after two road agents grabbed the lead horses, but Richard Shortz, Clement's right hand man, lay dead with a bullet in his stomach.

The deputy sheriff threw down his gun, but only after Clem guaranteed no passengers would be injured. The bandits got the money they were after and the stage was ordered on its way. The outlaws buried Shortz by the trail and then headed back to Virginia City, arriving before sunrise.

Nobody suspected them to be the stage robbers. After all, to cover such a distance in the amount of time they did was almost impossible to the imagination.

A woman passenger told the deputy sheriff about the wheel mark on the overcoat, and posses searched near and far for the coat.

A man on C Street in Virginia City was spotted with the wanted item and the Sheriff commenced questioning him. It turned out that he had loaned the overcoat to Clement Lee. The highwayman and his cohorts were rounded up in a manner of minutes.

Before being imprisoned in Nevada State Prison, Lee admitted to being the runaway son of a divorced Washington millionaire. It seems he had attempted to reach his fathers level in society on his own. If he had not borrowed an overcoat for his last robbery, Clement Lee might have attained his desired status.

XXV

CAPISTRANO LOPEZ
He Was A Traitor To His People

Not much is known about Capistrano Lopez, except that he might be considered the Benedict Arnold of the Spanish Forces. Lopez was a sergeant in the Spanish troops, and was ordered by General Jose Castro to keep a close watch on Captain John C. Fremont's men in the Gavilan Peak area. Capistrano was to report to General Castro all of Fremont's movements.

Lopez, however, rode straight into the Fremont camp and told the American General what his orders were. In return he expected a few pesos. Fremont paid off the traitor, who then left for a career of rustling cattle near Natividad in 1846.

Capistrano was quite successful in his new business until he "branched out" and made a fatal mistake. Lopez killed and robbed Governor Manuel Micheltorena's personal messenger, who was going to Monterey with a bag of 800 dollars to pay Presidio soldiers.

The Governor's soldiers easily tracked down Lopez and exchanged several well-positioned pieces of lead for the bag of valuables in Capistrano's possession.

XXVI

WILLIAM MAYFIELD
He Killed In Self Defense

Nineteenth Century lawmen got their man more times than not; but the sheriff of Washoe County, Nevada, intentionally looked the other way when he spotted a convicted killer in 1862.

But the sheriff was not really to be blamed, because most people in Washoe and Ormsby Counties sympathized with Georgia-born William Mayfield.

Gambler Mayfield had gotten into a jam for letting his Southern feelings about the Civil War be known in the presence of Northern sympathizers.

This unhealthy habit caused him to get in several fights with Yankees, and eventually with John Blackburn, a former United States Marshal. Blackburn, who was Sheriff of Ormsby County in 1862, had strong contempt for Southerners.

When he heard Mayfield praising the South during a poker game, the whiskey-lubricated sheriff told the Confederate to go for his gun. Mayfield, knowing Blackburn's reputation with a hogiron, dropped his gunbelt and a fist fight ensued. During the rough-and-tumble affair, Blackburn was getting hit pretty hard, and he reached for his gun to finish off the Southerner. As he did so, Mayfield pulled a knife and stabbed the sheriff in the heart.

The murderer was arrested and soon convicted by a jury made up of Yankee sympathizers. Mayfield was sent to the state prison in Carson City until his appeal could be heard by a higher court.

Most of the residents in Washoe and Ormsby counties felt that Mayfield had killed in self-defense, according to newspaper accounts.

One of these sympathizers smuggled some tools into Mayfield. With the tools, Mayfield was able to loosen the bars on his window, and that night he escaped to Huffaker's Station near Reno where he had friends who would hide him.

Most people in Washoe County, Nevada, knew where Mayfield was—at his girlfriend's house—but nobody spoke of it in public.

Finally, the new sheriff thought he had better make a quick look for Mayfield, so that state authorities would not think him negligent in his duties.

The sheriff and his posse went to the girlfriend's home, and during a routine search, they spotted Mayfield's boots behind his girlfriend's dresses in the closet. The lawmen quickly made an abrupt about face and left the home for Reno "showing disappointment" that they had not located the killer.

Meanwhile, Mayfield left with his girlfriend for Boise, Idaho, where he spent the remainder of his life as a miner—forever thankful to the understanding Nevadans who had saved his neck.

XXVII

VICTOR MONCAGA
He Hung Around Unwillingly

New Year's Eve was celebrated pretty much the same throughout the Mother Lode and Comstock Lode. Drinking, eating, playing poker, chasing dance hall girls, and just plain having a good time—whooping it up—describes a typical celebration in the 1870's. And such was the case in Columbus, Nevada on the New Year's Eve of 1873.

Everyone was having a good time, and the whole town turned out for the festivities. A big dance hall was the main center of attraction in Columbus. For this one day, amnesty was granted to criminals as everybody helped get the New Year off to a fresh start.

One bad egg, unknown in these parts, was Victor Moncaga, a cold-blooded killer who rode into Columbus a day before the lawmen who were after him. Victor was not one to lose out on a good thing, and when he saw that booze and eats were offered free he stopped his flight long enough to partake in the celebration.

Moncaga immediately took to liking a Chilean woman named Rosita, who ignored Vic's advances, preferring instead to play her guitar. Victor was not one to be ignored, and in a rage the outlaw grabbed Rosita's guitar and smashed it into many pieces.

Antonio Rivera, a gentleman standing near Rosita, objected to Moncaga's actions. Victor pulled out a bowie knife and put a slit across Antonio's throat, then fled out the door and stole a horse.

The Sheriff, who was in the dance hall at the time, pursued Victor and fired a round over the badman's head. Moncaga cowardly dropped his gun and knife before being escorted to the Columbus Jail.

The easy-going, fun-loving crowd took on a changed appearance following the brutal murder of popular Antonio Rivera. Quickly they worked up a scheme by which the killer would meet justice that very night.

74

Creating a diversion which sent the Sheriff to the far end of the city, the vigilantes removed Moncaga from the pokey and took him to the opposite end of town where the cattle slaughtering grounds stood.

There the screaming murderer was placed on the windlass, which up to that time had been used to hoist only beef carcasses. The mob then went back to the dance hall and once again joined in the celebration.

Meanwhile the Columbus Sheriff returned from the false alarm and was informed that Victor had been dealt with by vigilante hands. The law officer realized there was nothing further he could do, so he rejoined the festivity.

Later that night two men were sent to pull Moncaga's body down and bury it. The horrified vigilantes discovered that Victor was still struggling, so they returned to the hall and reported that it was too dark for them to see the body.

On New Years Day an official coroner's jury went out to the slaughter house and pronounced Victor Moncaga to be "very dead." That same afternoon two deputy sheriffs rode into Columbus in search of Moncaga. It seems the badman had committed several other murders in Southern California, and a $2,000 reward was offered for his capture, dead or alive.

The Sheriff produced the body and accepted the reward money on the town's behalf. Ironically, the money was used to build a more secure jail.

As for Victor Moncaga—he should not have looked a gift horse in the mouth. Since he did, the people of Columbus were forced to make Vic "hang around" and die a most painful death.

XXVIII

HANK PARRISH
His Bad Hand of Poker Proved Fatal

Hank Parrish was a murderer—but only when he thought he had to be. Eighteen times he decided a mans fate, usually after losing heavily in a poker game. For awhile Parrish lived in Tin Tac, Utah, but when the law finally located him, Hank "migrated" to Pioche, Nevada.

In the rip-roaring town of Pioche, Parrish showed signs of turning over a new leaf. Hank took on a job as a carpenter; and his new friends saw him as a respectable, hard-working westerner.

All went well in the life of Parrish until the evening of August 2, 1890, when he sat down for a friendly game of poker with his peers at James Curtis' Saloon in Jackrabbit, a few miles North of Pioche.

His old obsession of having to win once again got the best of him. After losing both money and temper, Hank accused popular P. G. Thompson of cheating. Without giving advance notice, Hank leaped across the table and stabbed Thompson fatally in the chest. Parrish was subdued by onlookers and turned over to the Jackrabbit Sheriff.

Fearing a lynching before trial, the veteran lawman moved his prisoner to the Ely Jail. On December 11, 1890 the Ely jury found Hank guilty of murder. Two days later the former Utah gambler was hanged, but not before confessing that his wife was not destitute as rumored, but had died years before, after giving him two lovely daughters. Following the hanging Hank's body was exhibited for two hours in the courthouse, as a reminder to potential lawbreakers to live within the law.

XXIX

LANGFORD PEEL
He Was Forced Into Becoming Chief

Some people do not want to be in a certain profession but fate guides them into it anyway. Such was the case of Langford Peel, a law abiding Nevada farmer who wanted to live in peace.

Peel owned a small settlement outside of Virginia City and used his gun only occasionally—and only to protect himself and his property from wild animals.

Unfortunately for Langford word of his "fast draw" grew out of an incident in which he killed a "cat" who had leaped on him unexpectantly. A friend of his, who had witnessed the event, "stretched the truth" a little while telling a mutual acquaintance about the tale. Before long Virginia City was "buzzing" with the news about a new "Chief."

The oldtimers discounted the yarn for they had never seen the blonde-bearded, rosy-cheeked Langford use his guns—or even wear them for that matter. But the young toughs, always out to show their ignorance, took particular notice of the gossip.

A couple of days later a nogood big mouth, who called himself El Dorado Johnny, strolled confidently into Pat Lynches Saloon on C Street, where Langford had gone for a snort. Johnny walked up to the bar and insisted on fighting Peel, who reluctantly obliged by following El Dorado out into the street.

Johnny proved fast, but Langford was faster. Peel felt sorry about the affair and even paid funeral expenses; but the deed had been done, and soon all of El Dorado's fellow punks were looking for Langford.

One by one they were buried alongside Johnny in Flowery Hill Cemetery, and Langford's abilities with a shooting iron were talked about from Denver to Gold Hill. It was said that Peel's secret in gunfighting was to shoot first, and that his Golden Rule was, "Do unto others as they would do unto you—only do it first."

Most Virginia City citizenry felt that Peel was doing a good thing by ridding the town of ruffians; but a small segment of the populace demanded that justice be done, and before long Langford Peel was taken forcefully by a vigilante mob before Judge Davenport.

At first the Judge sentenced him to twenty days in jail plus $100, but later he released Peel on the gunslinger's recognizance and promise to reappear in court at a later date.

The next afternoon, Langford, true to his word, appeared outside the chin-whiskered Judge's court. Without explaining his actions, Peel barged into the courtroom, where a trial was being held, and walked straight up to Judge Davenport.

The gunslinger grabbed the Judge's beard and repeatedly banged Davenport's head against a table. Lawmen stood in shock nearby, unwilling to interfere with "Chief" Peel.

Needless to say, the Langford Peel Case was closed, and the man who was forced into becoming a desperado left for Helena, Montana where he had friends. There he lived on his gunfighting tales before being shot in the back by a two-bit nobody. Carved on his tombstone, as he desired, was the following epitaph: "I know that my redeemer liveth." This is interpreted by historians to mean that Langford's redeemer is the man who would avenge his death.

Thus ends the saga of one of the Far West's fastest guns who was thought to have been a Harvard graduate that came West to strike it rich. He should have stuck to his books.

XXX

RICHARD PERKINS
He Could Only Ride an Iron Horse

In 1915 a five-foot-nine, stocky, bearded man named Richard Perkins was in charge of the Kentucky State exhibit in the Panama-Pacific International Exposition in San Francisco.

Few people recognized the honorable gentleman, who thirty-five years earlier had been one of California's most hunted highwaymen.

Richard Perkins, alias Dick Fellows, alias George Little, was in and out of California jails for more than thirty years. The reason for his misfortune of always getting caught, lay around the fact that no matter how hard he tried, Perkin's just did not have whatever it took to be a successful stage robber.

A lot of the trouble centered around his inability to stay on a horse. No matter what horse he tried to ride, the critter would either throw him off or take him in the wrong direction.

In 1875 Perkins attempted to rob his first stage. As he ordered the Concord to stop near Santa Barbara, Richard's hired horse bucked him to the ground.

For his efforts he was captured and received a three year stay in the pokey.

Fresh out of jail, using the name Dick Fellows, he once again tried to hold up a stage. This time as he approached the halted coach Dick's rented horse sent him head over heals, rendering him unconscious.

When he came to his senses the stage was well on its way to Bakersfield. "Never say die" must have been Fellows' battle cry, because a few days later, riding a stolen horse, he went back to meet the same stage.

At last the robbery went like clockwork—well, almost like clockwork. Dick got a strongbox, but once again lacking the know-how of a polished road agent, he forgot to bring anything with which to open the iron chest.

Always resourceful, Fellows tried to tie the box on his horse. The animal reared and took off on a gallop. Hiding his box, Dick "borrowed" a horse from the barn of a Bakersfield farm. This mare just happened to lose a shoe, which enabled the law to locate the hardluck highwayman.

Escaping from a temporary jailhouse by making a hole in the wall, the elusive road agent headed north. Dick spotted a horse near the barn of a ranch, but when he went over to mount it, much to his dismay, he discovered that the animal had no saddle. Finally finding a saddle in a vacated barn, Fellows approached the horse only to have it run off.

One way or another he managed to make his way to Santa Cruz, where, for some strange reason, he took up an honest job. In the Spring of 1881, Dick worked as a solicitor for the *Daily Echo* newspaper.

Attempting to make more money while going "straight" he placed an ad in the paper calling himself "George Little, professor of languages."

He offered to teach foreign languages in Santa Cruz, though few, if any, answered his ad. Evidentally dismayed with honest work, Dick Fellows went back to his prior job.

In the summer of 1881, he twice successfully liberated the San Luis Obispo to Soledad Stage of its valuables.

Fellows then proceeded northward holding up the stage running from Duncan Mills to Point Arena. But once again, lacking the skill of a veteran highwayman, he forgot that the strongbox was not delivered on Monday, and he ended up with a box that newspaper reporters said contained one letter written in Chinese.

At this time posters went up around the Bay Area offering $600 reward for the capture of Fellows. In January of 1882, over sixty lawmen searched between Santa Cruz and San Francisco for the stage menace.

One Palo Alto woman said she had served Dick a meal, not knowing he was an outlaw. He told her all about the bad Dick Fellows and how he was going to hunt down the road agent, she explained to the local sheriff.

80

On January 28, 1882 Dick was captured in Mayfield without a fight and without a horse. Santa Clara Constable Arnold Burke was given custody of the outlaw for delivery to San Jose, where Fellows was to be transported by train to a Santa Barbara jail.

Proud of his now infamous prisoner, Burke carelessly accepted Dick's suggestion for a "last drink" in San Jose's IXL Saloon, near First Street.

Showing his "catch" off to his friends in the bar, Burke had a little too much to drink. Leaving the bar, Fellows belted Burke with his handcuffs and fled, finally ending up in a barn just outside of San Jose, near Santa Clara College.

Dr. Matthew Gunckel, the ranch owner, found Dick sleeping beside an empty wine bottle in his barn. Clever-thinking Fellows presented the sob story of his life about how he was a "down and out" drunk who had escaped prison. The sympathetic doctor gave the poor soul some clothes before sending him on his way.

Meanwhile a massive manhunt was combing the Santa Clara County hillsides for the escaped bandit. On February 3, 1882, San Jose Police got word that a man fitting Fellow's description had been spotted near Los Gatos.

The next day, Police Chief Dan Haskell, who was searching the Los Gatos foothills with a dozen deputies, spied Dick eating in a cabin of an unsuspecting family. Somehow the highwayman had gotten rid of his handcuffs.

The horseless bandit was hauled off peacefully to the San Jose Jail where he enjoyed becoming an overnight celebrity, much as infamous outlaw Tiburcio Vasquez had, seven years earlier.

Over seven hundred people came from throughout the valley to see the much-talked-about road agent. Like Vasquez, Fellows welcomed conversation with all who wished to speak through the jail bars. He politely discussed every aspect of his career as a bandit, much to the pleasure of the public.

After a few days, Dick was transferred to San Francisco, then south to Santa Barbara, where, once again, he attempted

81

to escape. Knocking down a jail guard, Fellows ran outside only to end up in a street gutter—victim of a bucking stolen horse.

Ironically, in a letter to the Santa Barbara Press, with no mention of horses, Dick had told of his dealings with crime: "My unfortunate experience has thrown me into the society of thousands of lawbreakers in all walks of life and in every instance the result is the same sad story. It don't pay."

On March 7, 1908, Lt. Gov. Porter pardoned the thirty-six-year-old stage robber. Dick left Folsom Prison for his native Kentucky.

Noted Wells Fargo Detective James B. Hume was interviewed about Fellows by a San Francisco Examiner reporter.

"For daring he is the equal of any outlaw with whom I have ever had dealings," said Hume. "His nerve, morally and physically, is superb, his resource in hours of peril is apparently inexhaustible and his ability, natural and acquired, would have made him as great in any honest profession he might have chosen."

Though somewhat late in life, Richard Perkins, alias Dick Fellows, finally saw the light. From one of California's most unusual highwaymen he became influential in Kentucky politics.

In 1915 he revisited California with a position of honor—in charge of representing his home state of Kentucky in the Panama-Pacific International Exposition in San Francisco.

Somewhat ironically, the distinguished representative came to the Golden State from Kentucky riding an iron horse.

XXXI

SALOMON PICO
The Governor's Cousin Was a Killer

Salomon Pico was of aristocratic background. He was the cousin of California Governor Pico and General Andres Pico, and the brother of Don Jose Jesus Pico, grantee of the Rancho, now known as Hearst Ranch at San Simeon. Rather than being a rancher himself, Salomon thought it best to be a killer.

Pico's career of robbery and murder centered around his absolute hatred of Americanos. He was a cowardly killer who never attacked his victims in the open, but always at night in the back country along El Camino Real.

His method of attack was to ambush individuals, knifing them in the back. Out of fear many Californians gave Pico food and lodging, thus allowing the murderer safe passage from one valley to another. This was not an uncommon service given to early outlaws; but unlike earlier bandits, Salomon Pico was politically motivated.

In anger over a court's decision against Californians in 1850, Pico nearly assassinated Judge Benjamin Hayes in Los Angeles on November 12, 1851. Pico was a bit off target and his thrown knife felled Hayes' assistant. Salomon was quickly grabbed by lawmen, but because of his political ties the coldblooded killer was exiled to Lower California where he served as a bodyguard for exiled General Jose Castro.

The outlaw was eventually shot and killed by Governor Esparza in 1860. It seems that Esparza had a personal revenge justification for this act since, Pico had killed his uncle.

XXXII

POMPONIO
Terror Was His Calling Card

February 6, 1824 marks the death of one of California's earliest highwaymen. On this date the notorious Pomponio was "done in" by his own gang of desperadoes.

For two years, 1823-1824, Pomponio and his brigade of Indian highwaymen terrorized the countryside from Sonora to Santa Cruz, killing fellow Indians and looting anything of value in the area.

As is the case with many criminals, nobody knows why Pomponio, a one-time neophyte of Mission San Francisco (Dolores) turned to a profession of murder. He was so mean that even his own men were terrorized of him.

Two of Pomponio's chief lieutenants, Gonzalo (formerly from Mission Carmel) and Baltaser (from Soledad) wanted to retire from the gang and try living a peaceful life, but they knew they could not face their maker before turning their leader in. The alert Pomponio got wind of the situation and tied his two lieutenants to a stake, then set the stake afire.

This action brought a rebellion in the ranks, and the leaders own cohorts did away with him by knifing him with his own blade.

XXXIII

THOMAS BELL POOLE
He Swung With Rebel Robin Hoods

It was noon on September 29, 1865 in Placerville, California. The blue skies covered the silence of a large gathering on Main Street. The occasion—Thomas Bell Poole, former undersheriff of Monterey County was about to be hanged.

Poole had been part of a scheme, originating in Santa Clara County, to recruit and equip soldiers in California for the Confederate Army.

To get the needed financing for such a project, the Southern sympathizers in Northern California secretly formed a Confederate company of soldiers, which held up stages from the Pacific Coast to the Mother Lode.

Modeled after Quantrill's Blood Raiders in Kansas, each of the sixteen-member company swore never to be taken alive. Much of the membership came from Monterey, Santa Cruz, and Santa Clara Counties.

A secluded spot near the Mount Hamilton Range served as the headquarters for the Confederates who menaced ranchers, mule trains, stages, and lone travelers from May to October of 1864.

There was such a fear of the rebels in San Jose that word was spread by city officials to sleep with reliable weapons within reach.

Luckily for the citizens of San Jose, the favorite stomping ground of the Confederates was the Mother Lode, where gold shipments were plentiful. There they would waylay a coach and come back to San Jose until things quieted down.

On the dark night of June 30, 1864, the Southern Robin Hoods successfully performed one of the biggest stickups in Western history. Six road agents, wearing full Confederate uniforms, stopped the Lake Tahoe to Placerville Stage as it slowed down for the narrow curve at Bullion Bend, thirteen miles from Hangtown.

With courtesy seldom used by highwaymen, one soldier —ranked Captain—explained to the passengers the reason their coach was halted. "Ladies and gentlemen, we are not robbers but a company of Confederate soldiers here not to harm or steal from you. All we want is the Wells Fargo treasure to assist us in our recruitment for the Confederate Army."

No sooner had the Captain finished his explanation, when out of the silent night, a clatter of hoofbeats was heard. Around the bend came a second stage, this one from Virginia City. Apparently unaware of the holdup in progress, the second Concord came to a stop.

Three rebels surrounded the new arrival while the Captain gave the first driver a receipt which said: "This is to certify that I have received from Wells Fargo and Co. the sum of XXX cash, for the purpose of outfitting recruits enlisted in California for the Confederate States Army."

The note was signed by Captain R. H. Ingrim, Company G, Confederate States of America, detached duty. Elated over the two stage treasures for the price of one hold up, Captain Ingrim forgot to fill in the amount of cash taken.

The first stagewhip was told "to make the dust fly," as the rebels proceeded to strip the second Concord of its valuables. In all, $20,000 in coin and eight sacks of gold bullion were "borrowed" for the Confederate cause.

The Southern Robin Hoods divided the loot, then left in different directions, with plans of meeting in San Jose a week later.

One of Jefferson Davis' boys did not make out so well. Thomas Bell Poole, foolishly lodging near the scene of the crimes, was shot by a Sheriff's Deputy and taken to a Placerville jail. There, after he was identified by two stage drivers, Poole told in detail all he knew about the gang. From this information authorities were able to recover five sacks of bullion.

Meanwhile, four of the bandits returned to San Jose, where they stashed some of the bullion in the Almaden hills. Striking while their luck was still with them, these rebels robbed two stages on the outskirts of San Jose, once again hiding the valuables in the Almaden hills.

On July 15, 1864, three Confederates left their hideout for Almaden, where they planned to lay in wait for the stage with the New Almaden Mine payroll. The bandits, playing the role of visitors to the area, stopped at the Hill Ranch, two and a half miles South of San Jose on the New Almaden Road.

They asked Rancher Hill if they could stay overnight in the barn. The hospitable rancher readily agreed and invited the men to dinner. Later that evening, the rebels, saturated with success and whiskey, "spilled the beans" regarding who they were and what their plans were.

Hill slipped outside and rode into San Jose, where he reported the conversation of his guests to Sheriff John H. Adams. Sheriff Adams and a hastily recruited posse went to Hill's Ranch and surrounded the house.

As Adams approached the front door he was greeted with gunfire. A blazing gunbattle ensued, one which took the lives of a deputy and two rebels. Not living up to his solemn pledge, Alban Glasby meekly surrendered and led the lawmen to some of the hidden loot in the Almaden hills.

That same night another contingent of the gang was plotting the massacre of a pro-Union Almaden cavalry regiment, when Placerville Sheriff James B. Hume and his men closed in and arrested the twelve bandits.

Hume, using Poole's information, was able to locate this portion of the rebs, meeting in one of the members' South San Jose homes. These men were allegedly responsible for the burning down of the pro-Union Methodist Church at Berryessa.

The last of the Confederates to be arrested was John Grant, who, having successfully robbed two stages single-handedly near San Juan Batista, was captured by officers in a cabin near the Forbes Mill in Los Gatos. As is often the case with Far Western outlaws, Grant was betrayed by a jealous girlfriend.

Though most of the rebels were captured, all went free

on technicalities, with the exception of Preston Hodges, who received twenty years in San Quentin Prison, and Thomas Bell Poole, who was hanged as a warning to Confederate sympathizers to live within the law.

The Southern Robin Hoods were no longer a menace to California. The shoot-out at the Hill Ranch in San Jose was of historical significance since, it was the scene of the only Civil War "battle" fought in The Golden State.

XXXIV

JACK POWERS
The Hogs Got the Best of Him

Not very many badmen enjoyed the power that Jack Powers did in the 1850's. For three years he built a virtual one-man syndicate, controlling over 400 gamblers in Los Angeles. But Powers was not a man to sit still, so he left his position of power and headed North where he started a remarkable career of robbery.

He reportedly robbed more cattle-buyers in the San Francisco area than did other outlaws operating in the Golden State. Once again, not desiring to remain idle, Jack left his budding business and returned to Los Angeles. After all, it was there that he was mustered out of Stevenson's Regiment and became a ranch-hand, before pursuing a career of crime.

Jack decided to get together a crew of cutthroats, who would enable him to increase his already impressive wealth. Part of his success resulted from Powers' recruiting of two men who looked identically like him. This allowed for parts of his gang to hit all over the state, at the same time, thus having lawmen believe that each crime was the job of Jack Powers.

The headquarters for the gang was the Santa Ynez Valley, where the Jack Powers group robbed, looted, killed and burned. Even lawmen were afraid, with just cause, to enter the valley which was labeled "Jack Powers Graveyard."

Slowly but surely "Jackie's" gang got whittled down, basically due to inward quarrels over women and over the division of loot. In 1857 Jack Powers and the last member of his band of cutthroats, Rafael Monea, fatally stabbed each other in a fight in lower California.

Their bodies were discovered in a farmer's hogpen, half eaten by hogs. Quite a fitting end for one of California's worst outlaws.

XXXV

SUSAN RAPER
She Was Queen of Cattle Rustlers

Charm was what Susan Raper possessed—that is, along with good looks. Using this charm Susan was able to become one of the West's biggest cattle rustlers, to avoid prison sentences, and to gain an enormous wealth.

Mrs. Raper turned to crime out of necessity. Along with her husband, three sons and brother, Susan came to Nevada from New South Wales, Australia when she was twenty-nine-years-old. The Rapers wanted to be ranchers, but renegade Indians killed the rest of her family, leaving Susan badly injured and without a home.

Sue was taken in by a stage bandit, recently retired, and his wife, who were barely eeking out an existence as subsistence farmers. It was from the former road agent, Jess Wright, that she learned how profitable crime had been for him years before.

The recent widow began thinking about her possible qualities as an outlaw. She could shoot a rifle like a marksman, ride a horse like an Indian, and she possessed a good, clever mind capable of planning robberies. Yet for some unknown reason, Mrs. Raper put her talents together and became a cattle rustler instead of stage robber.

She recruited a gang of ten shady men who learned to respect her rifle when thinking about her charm. Together the Raper gang rustled cattle along the Humboldt River and in the Pine, Crescent, and Reese River Areas. They changed the brand on the stolen cattle and built up quite a herd for the Raper Ranches at Carlin and Elko. Throughout the 1860's cattlemen were plagued by the female cattle rustler, and several thousand dollars were offered for her capture.

Thrice she was arrested by sheriff's posses, and three times she was freed by the twelve-man jury, who refused to send such a charming lady to prison. The next time she was arrested, a not-so-lenient jury of cattlemen convicted her, and she was sentenced to a ten-year prison term. True to form, Susan charmed the jailkeeper into her cell, where she hit him on the head with a stool and escaped.

The Cattle Rustling Queen went to New Mexico, where she settled in Socorro and bought a saloon. It was in her saloon that she charmed a wealthy widower, George Black, who just happened to own the largest spread in the area. Black married Susan and put her name as chief beneficiary in his will.

Then one day when George returned from town, Susan Raper gunned him down. A tough New Mexico jury, not the least impressed with her charm, placed the Australian emigrant behind bars for the rest of her life. The Queen of Nevada Cattle Rustlers had stolen her last cow.

XXXVI

ANNE RICHEY
Pain Was the Price She Paid

Western historians have never been able to figure out what made beautiful Anne Richey turn to a career of crime in Wyoming. This tragic story starts in 1919, when Miss Richey used to help her wealthy cattleman father in round-ups on their Kemmerer ranch.

The clever cowgirl easily picked up the skills of roping and branding; and her friends later reported that she was as good with her gun as any of her father's hired ranch hands.

Her father, however, was happy when Anne finally decided to settle down and marry the Kemmerer school superintendent, because he thought a womans place was in a home raising children. But after a few months of marriage, Anne grew tired of being a housewife, and she left her husband to work with a former acquaintance, Charles King.

With King, Miss Richey went back to her real love—the cattle business. The two lovers purchased a small ranch and commenced "acquiring" cattle by rounding up strays from other rancher's herds.

Miss Richey then brandblotted the stolen steers and sent them to Omaha, where King sold them to the highest bidder. This profitable business flourished for several months, until Anne was finally caught in the act with the merchandise by a local deputy sheriff.

A jury acquitted King for lack of evidence; but Miss Richey was sentenced to one to six years in the state penitentiary. However, the Wyoming Penitentiary did not have facilities to accomodate women; and authorities agreed to have Anne serve her sentence in the Colorado State Penitentiary.

Anne's attorney appealed the case, pleading that his client was not really as bad as she was made out to be. But the Wyoming Supreme Court upheld the conviction.

Miss Richey was given a few days to get her affairs in

order. On one of these days she was paid a visit by a tall man on an "iron-gray horse," according to Otto Palsenberger, who did odd jobs for Anne at her ranch.

Following the strange visit, Otto went into the ranchhouse to find out what was up. Anne said the stranger was just "an old friend," and she asked Palsenberger to take off his hat and eat lunch with her.

Anne sat down at the table and started eating beef stew. Moments later she fell to the floor in convulsions and died. Otto, who had eaten only one mouthful of stew, also fell to the floor in agony, but he later recovered.

Authorities concluded that while Anne was talking with the stranger, another man poisoned her stew, although the autopsy was unable to reveal what type of poison had been used.

One Wyoming paper blamed her death on another member of her cattle rustling gang because "no woman could have done all that rustling without a gang . . ."

Theorized the Wyoming State Tribune, "She was probably murdered so she wouldn't reveal her partners in crime."

Anne Richey, the only woman ever convicted of cattle rustling by a Wyoming jury, learned in a painful way that "crime don't pay."

XXXVII

NICKANOR RODRIGUEZ
Nevada's Dr. Jeckyll-Mr. Hyde

Nickanor Rodriguez was a popular figure in the Comstock Lode during the 1860's. He lived in a mansion and had a wide reputation as an affluent mining man who threw the most lavish dinner parties around. Among Nick's friends were the most influential people in Virginia City. Judges, bank owners, and, of course, beautiful women enjoyed the company of the young, handsome, articulate bachelor.

Rodriguez had a distinguished background. His father was an important government official in Spain; and as a youth Nick had the pleasure of visiting Rome, Paris and Mexico before deciding to live in the United States.

Nick was certainly a first-rate citizen—or at least his acquaintances thought so. Little did his friends know that the real Nickanor Rodriguez was Nevada's most ruthless outlaw.

When he was not entertaining high society, he was stealing amalgam and silver right out of the Comstock mines, robbing Wells Fargo stages, sticking up banks, or killing partners and people slow to turn over their cash.

The two-faced criminal started his lawless career at the tender age of sixteen when, feeling a lust for excitement, he joined up with an outlaw gang in Tuolumne County, Calif.

Following an unsuccessful bank robbery, the gang was tracked down by the sheriff's posse. Nick was sentenced to ten years in jail, but after serving one year he was pardoned by the Governor because of his youth.

Not learning his lesson, Nick went to Nevada and posed as a remittance man, an occupation which enabled him to meet and mingle with wealthy people. Meanwhile, behind the scenes, he rounded up a motley crew of cutthroats who proceeded to rob nearly every mill in Nevada.

Several times the unguarded Imperial Mill and Pacific

Mill, in Gold Hill, were robbed, and each time the bullion was buried outside the Silver City Cemetery. A few weeks later, Rodriguez returned to the graveyard and transformed the bullion into bars, whereupon he would sell them.

At the same time, the Nickanor Rodriguez whom Virginia City "society-elite" knew, continued to gain in popularity, throwing parties that were hard to equal. He was able to live his double life by telling his acquaintances that he had to go out of state on business, sometimes for weeks at a time.

Nick was never placed under suspicion by his wealthy friends, even though stage robberies and quartz mine riflings became increasing occurrances during his absence.

Cleverness and poise were two virtues that enhanced Rodriguez' occupation. One day the alert outlaw saw three large gold bricks being loaded under the front boot on the Virginia City-Reno Stage. Nick bought a ticket for Reno and calmly sat down on the box next to famed stagewhip Baldy Green. When Green stopped to water the horses near Steamboat Springs, Nick threw the gold bricks into the brush. He remained in his seat until the stage got to Reno.

Rodriguez then rented a buggy and went back for the loot. He did slip up though, as he left the bricks at the assay office to be appraised, and the suspicious merchant notified the Sheriff. The lawmen staked out the office; but Nick, who had been tipped off by one of his informants, never came to pick up the bricks.

Rather upset at his bungling of the affair, Nickanor headed for Eastern Nevada until things cooled off. There, Nick and a couple members from his gang robbed White Pine County's Shermantown Mill of bullion.

In an all out effort to "nail" the bandit who was seriously harassing Nevada, posses totaling 250 men searched White Pine County for the desperadoes. It was not long before Nick was tracked down and escorted to jail.

He was not there long, as his close friend and fellow socialite, Judge Jesse Pitzer, managed to get him acquitted.

"After all," Judge Pitzer told the jury, "a man of Rodriguez' stature does not go around robbing, let alone associating with hoodlums."

Following his release, Nick "layed low" for a couple of months, throwing his enormous bashes for the socially prominent in Virginia City. Local papers also praised his large contribution to charity.

In July he left the Comstock to return to his old business. Once again he joined his gang of outlaws at their hideout at Devil's Gate—outside of Silver City—and they began holding up Wells Fargo coaches. They were so successful at this livelihood that Wells Fargo stagelines did not dare ship strongboxes of value in the Rodriguez "controlled" areas of the state.

In fact, Wells Fargo was so shook up that it paid Nick $2,000 a month not to rob their stages. The criminal master sent a representative to allegedly sign a contract with a Wells Fargo branch representative, promising that Nick's gang would not "bother" the Wells Fargo Stages. He instructed his proxy to write into the contract, "In a transaction of this kind either side should be free to terminate the agreement at will."

True to his word, Rodriguez stopped robbing Wells Fargo strongboxes and went back to hosting some of the wildest parties in the history of Comstock mining. Imported French wine, champagne, and wild game were consumed on the Rodriguez grounds in the course of an evening.

Each night a different woman would be seen hanging on the handsome bachelor-bandit's arm. They each dreamed of marriage, but Nick had far more important matters on his mind.

He mingled socially with the rich for one reason and one reason only—that was to find out what mills would be left unguarded, and when; what large bullion shipments would be made by stage, and to where; and which bank vaults deserved breaking into.

After receiving the desired information he would always leave town on business. During one party Nick learned that the Wells Fargo stageline had assumed new ownership. The next morning the new owners were notified, by an unsigned telegram, that the contract would no longer be honored.

The Rodriguez gang continued their stage holdups until, at another dinner, Nick heard about how well the Nevada State Bank was doing and what new security procedures were being made to prevent stickups.

With this new tidbit, Nick's band started becoming involved in bank robberies. In consecutive hold ups they got over $10,000 in coin from the Nevada State Bank. Determined posses finally caught up with the Spanish bandit in Austin. Rodriguez was thrown into the pokey and as a security measure, three guards were placed inside the Sheriff's office and two lawmen patrolled outside.

This time eyewitnesses verified that Nick was the desperado who had been plaguing Nevada. The outlaw's society friends must have been overcome with shock and disbelief. "There will be no more wild game and champagne dinners for Nickanor," wrote one newsman. The bandit, regarded by several historians as the "King of the Nevada Desperadoes," was sentenced to life imprisonment. His gang, however, remained loyal and freed him from lawmen while Nick was being transported to prison.

Rodriguez went to Utah for awhile and stayed at the ranch of James Maxwell, who was wanted for murder in Nevada. Maxwell, Nick, and a French killer named Eugene Billieu, returned to Nevada one last time and successfully waylaid the Pioche Stage before the threesome went to Mexico.

The last known act of Nickanor Rodriguez' lengthy "Dr. Jekyll-Mr. Hyde" career was to shoot his two partners in the back at the Mexican border. He then took the money and moved to Sinaloa, Mexico, where he bought a large horse ranch and became known as Don Felipe Castro, one of Mexico's largest landowners.

True to form, he was socially accepted by the aristocrats as well as the senoritas. Contrary to an earlier newsman's belief, Nickanor Rodriguez, alias Don Felipe Castro, once again threw wild game and champagne dinners.

Historians do not record if he ever returned to crime; but it must be remembered that his intention in throwing parties was to gain information which he could use in his career as an outlaw.

If Nick "got wind of" a bank bulging with money or a stage loaded with bullion, one can place a good bet on the Spanish bandit coming out of "retirement." After all, Rodriguez did not earn his title, "King of Nevada Desperadoes," by sitting still.

XXXVIII

JOHN and CHARLES RUGGLES
They Were Hanged Side By Side

John and Charles Ruggles always wanted to be a successful brother team. They bought a blacksmith shop near Sacramento and worked hard, but eventually had to sell out for a sizeable loss. They next bought a small grocery store, but could not make a go of it. They then tried their hand at gold panning, but they were forty years too late.

One would think they would get the message and go off on their separate ways. Unfortunately for them they did not. Finding that honest work got them nowhere, the Ruggles Brothers turned to a career of crime. They hoped to be a successful outlaw team, but, as in their other business ventures, they somehow lacked the knowhow.

In January of 1892 John and Charles Ruggles made plans to hold up the Wells Fargo Stage on its way to Whiskeytown, north of Redding, California. But the inexperienced would-be robbers accidentally selected the wrong trail, and the noon stage never did pass their way.

This did not discourage the Ruggles Brothers, who were used to getting "the short end of the stick." They merely made more detailed plans for a stage robbery.

John and Charles waited patiently until July, when a large shipment of gold was placed on the stage for Redding. This time they chose the right trail. The Ruggles, however, did not know that besides the $40,000 in gold bullion from The Trinity County Mines, the coach also carried famed Wells Fargo shotgun "Buck" Montgomery, who made a habit of personally seeing to it that the strongbox got to its desired destination.

As the Concord slowed down for a sharp curve on Middle Creek Road, the highwaymen, shotguns in hand, stood out in front of the horses and sounded the familiar cry, "Halt! Throw down your strongbox!"

These words set "Buck" Montgomery into action as he emptied both barrels at the brothers, who returned the fire. When the dust rose, John, Charles and driver John Boyce were injured, but "Buck" Montgomery was killed.

Severely-injured John Boyce managed to throw down the box before miraculously guiding the stage to a farm house. The Redding Sheriff was notified, and an angry posse got on the bandits trail at once.

It was but a few hours when they caught up with Charles Ruggles, who had lost so much blood that he had fallen off his horse into a ditch. He gave his name as Lee R. Howard, and claimed he had been involved in a hunting accident. He denied any part in the robbery. Unconvinced, the posse took their prisoner back to Redding.

The townspeople, who deeply admired "Buck" Montgomery, cried out for a lynching, but the Sheriff talked them out of it. Meanwhile, repeated searches by the posse failed to turn up Charles' partner. Rumors had it that he had fled North, toward Canada, with the loot.

A couple of days later, the break the lawmen had been waiting for occurred. A miner, calling himself Happy Hartman, was in town to buy supplies and he happened to peer in the window as he walked by the Sheriffs' office. Happy recognized Charles Ruggles and asked him about his brother. The prisoner continued to claim that his name was Howard.

Finally, after Happy told the Sheriff about a birthmark on Charles' right leg, the outlaw agreed that his name was Ruggles and that he had held up the stage. But Charles swore that he had not seen his brother for over twenty years.

The Sheriff did not buy this tale and got Happy to ded scribe John Ruggles. The next day "Wanted" posters were put up throughout the area, but John Ruggles was not to be found by posse or bounty hunter.

A couple of months after the robbery, the alert Woodland Constable, Wayne Wycoff, spotted a man that resembled John Ruggles' description, sitting in The Opera Restaurant.

Ruggles knew what the lawman was after and as soon as Wycoff entered the room, John attempted to flee out the back door. He was felled by a bullet in the shoulder.

John was transported back to Redding, where, once again, the Ruggles Brothers were brought together under something less than a joyful occasion. Neither of the highwaymen were willing to tell where they stashed the gold bullion, but they were always willing to spin yarns about how they had been the innocent sons of a well to do Arizona politician.

In fact, certain single women took pity on the "poor boys," and they brought the prisoners pies and cakes. The rest of the town, however, began talking "lynch." When word leaked out that the Ruggles had implicated popular "Buck" Montgomery as a culprit in the crime, a vicious mob that no Sheriff could control battered its way into the jail.

The outraged citizenry brought the terrorized John and Charles Ruggles outside to two nearby cottonwood trees. The brothers, realizing their predicament, offered to tell the mob where the loot was hidden in a trade for their lives.

The lynch mob could care less about the gold bullion. All they wanted was to hang the killers of "Buck" who had dared to tarnish the stage messenger's reputation. Without further adieu John and Charles Ruggles were hanged. A rather unsympathetic Wells Fargo Agent, James Hume, capped the case by saying, "They deserved their fate. I am very opposed to mob law and would rather have seen these men legally punished, but their crime was a most atrocious one and they were utterly undeserving of clemency."

The unsuccessful pair never achieved their desired status as a prosperous brother team, but then again, failure to attain goals was not an uncommon occurrence in rugged nineteenth-century California.

XXXIX

GEORGE SHANKS
Jack Williams' Ghost Became Just That

Jack Williams terrorized the Grass Valley-Nevada City area with his robberies in the early 1860's. Following one such holdup, Williams was captured and hanged. Yet, within the month a Jack Williams look-alike was robbing stages, prompting victims to call the new outlaw Jack Williams Ghost.

In actuality the highwayman was George Shanks, who had recently quit his job as a waiter in the Comptonville Hotel in hopes of making a few easy "bucks" in the rich Grass Valley area.

Following each stage robbery, Shanks took his loot to his hideout in a cave below a waterfall on the South Yuba River. Though stage jobs were his speciality, Shanks is remembered to historians for his humorous stickup of lone travelers along the road to the diggings of You Bet.

The segmented robbery started when a Chinaman walked into the shotgun-wielding Shanks' path. George ordered his first victim "to take a load off his feet" and sit on a gigantic fallen log on the path. Shanks and his victim sat on the log quietly until one by one a German, another Chinaman, an American and a Swede fell into the trap and were forced to join George on the log.

As Shanks was robbing his victims, another unfortunate, George Hilton, came stumbling along and enriched George's treasury by $60. Then, after having his victims lie face down on the dirt road, Shanks, alias Jack Williams Ghost, lived up to the latter name and disappeared into the brush.

It was not until May 15, 1866 that Shanks was seen again —as he held up a stage on the North grade of the road to Nevada City. The Ghost disappeared again, this time with $5,000 from the Wells Fargo strongbox. It was reported that before departing, George produced a bottle from his coat and gave all passengers and the driver a "shot of brandy."

After many months of searching for clues, Shanks was finally tracked down, due to the perseverance of Nevada City Sheriff Gentry who, along with his posse, accidentally discovered Shanks' hideaway.

A man of George's description had been seen near the South Yuba River and the posse covered every inch of the area. It was Steve Venard, a deputy, who climbed up a twenty-foot waterfall, thus coming face to face with the Ghost.

Without saying a word, Venard "drilled" Shanks, as well as his two partners, who must have died with a shocked look on their faces. For Venard's action, California Governor Frederick F. Low made Steve a lieutenant-colonel in the militia for "meritorious services in the field," and Wells Fargo gave the brave posseman a $3,000 reward and a new sixteen-shot Henry Rifle.

As for Jack Williams Ghost, he became just that.

XL

MILTON SHARP
He Believed That One Bad Habit Is Enough

Milton Anthony Sharp was the type of man daughters would have been proud to have brought home to their mothers. He neither drank, smoked, chewed tobacco nor used profanity. His charming manners and cultured use of the English language made him the target of many a female.

To "ice the cake," Sharp was of handsome appearance—five-foot-six; dark brown, wavy hair; broad shoulders; flashing brown eyes—enough so that his general carriage could have been mistaken for that of a diplomat or congressman.

But diplomat or congressman, Sharp was not. He had a far different occupation which was run in a courteous, orderly manner. Milton Anthony Sharp robbed stages. In fact, he was one of the most successful bandits in California as well as Nevada.

Nobody knows the reason this Missouri-born gentleman, who came to California to work in the mines, turned to crime. Between 1878 and 1880, Sharp held up fifteen stages, usually in the Bodie-Carson City area, where gold and silver from the Comstock was frequently transported.

Following each robbery he took the loot to his San Francisco home on Minna Street, where he lived in the greatest luxury available on the West Coast.

One of Sharp's victims in a Bodie Stage robbery, Colonel K. B. Brown of Nevada, told a San Francisco reporter: "I never knew anybody who could rob stages better than Sharp, not even barring Black Bart. He was one of the politest gentlemen I ever met. There was nothing vulgar or coarse about him. Everything was done in a business like way, and there was no unnecessary rudeness. He was particularly gallant to lady passengers and always acted like a high-toned gentleman." Sharp never resorted to violence, even when his partner was killed by a stage guard during one holdup.

Milton never encountered an empty strongbox, which indicates that he probably had inside information as to a stage's cargo.

The serious highwayman had the same *modus operandi* for each job. After halting the coach and taking the weapons from the guard and driver, Sharp politely ordered the passengers to line up with their hands in the air. Next, one by one, he turned their pockets inside out, letting their contents fall to the ground. The victims were then told to take three steps forward while Milton gathered the valuables, smashed open the strongbox, rifled the mail, and disappeared into the wilderness on horse.

Only once did the careful robber lose his stolen cargo. In February, 1880, he waylaid the Sacramento Stage on its way to Carson City. Sharp made off with $13,000 in gold notes from the Mills Bank of Sacramento.

With a posse not far behind, he buried the notes beneath some rocks near the South fork of the American River. A rancher stumbled upon the small fortune and used the gold notes to pay off the mortgage on his ranch.

Throughout 1880 "Wanted" posters with Sharp's description were a common sight around Northern California and Western Nevada. One Wells Fargo poster said Sharp was "about 45-years old, with a dark complexion, roman nose, scar on his right forearm and bright flashing eyes which he turns on you when he talks, never taking them away when conversing."

Despite widespread searching by lawmen, Sharp remained free, robbing six stages between May 15 and September 5, 1880. This frequency of holdup beat Black Bart's average on a per week basis.

Ironically, Milton's refusal to use aliases led to his downfall. On September 17, 1880 Wells Fargo Detective James Hume spotted a carpet bag with Sharp's name and address on it while in San Francisco's Market Street Depot. Hume staked out the Minna Street home and arrested Sharp when he returned that night from the Opera House.

Inside the valise Hume found $3,000 and a gold watch

from a recent robbery near Bodie. This evidence was enough to insure Milton a long stay in the pokey. Since the robbery occurred in Nevada, Sharp was transported to the Aurora Jail.

Having such a refined nature enabled Milton to talk the jailer into giving him a penknife for carving dolls out of wood for the jailer's children—a task which he performed to perfection. One November night he used the same knife to dig through the jail's stone and mortar to freedom.

The residents in the area surrounding Aurora were terrified. Wells Fargo, the town of Aurora, the County Commissioners, and the State of Nevada all offered rewards for the fugitive's capture.

A massive manhunt combed the area, as businessmen and miners joined lawmen in search of a man with a price on his head. As a precautionary measure, bullion shipments out of the Esmeralda region were suspended while Sharp was at large.

Milton was not to be found. What was found near Aurora was the Oregon Boot, a fifteen-pound steel shackle, which had been secured to his legs. This marked the first time in America that a man had freed himself from such a device.

A week later, Milton Sharp, nearly dead from starvation, turned himself in to the astonished sheriff in the Nevada town of Candelaria. Sharp would serve a five year term in the Nevada Penitentiary before being pardoned, never to return to crime again.

At the time of Sharp's "capture," Colonel Brown was asked by a San Francisco reporter why Milton had not stolen food, for if he had he would probably go free.

"Break into some ranch or miner's cabin? No, sir! Not in a hundred years. Milton A. Sharp was a stagerobber, but, sir, he would never stoop to burglary!"

XLI

FRANCISCO PANCHO SOTO
He Had a Lot Cooking Upstairs

Francisco Pancho Soto had the makings of an elite road agent. He was an excellent horseman, a fast man with a gun, possessed a mind fertile in resource, and he had friends throughout Northern California who put him up when posses closed in on him.

The tall, robust outlaw, with a full, flowing beard that gave him a benevolent appearance, also had a quick wit. With such traits Soto became an accomplished highwayman and enjoyed every minute of it. As he once told a newsman. "Robberies make my friends admire me for my courage and daring. I am never afraid. As for the money— it means nothing to me."

One day after relieving three men of their valuables, a posse led by the sheriffs from four counties, was "hot on his trail." As the sun set the lawmen stopped to rest in a Mexican casa in Livermore Valley. Soto (whose face was unknown to them) came to the door, whereupon a Sheriff asked if he had seen Pancho Soto. The outlaw replied, "I expect him here tomorrow at daylight." The happy sheriffs dismounted to spend the night in the house.

When they were fast asleep Soto took their weapons and valuables and stampeded their horses. The lawmen, upon hearing the whinnying, peered through the window to see Soto riding away, shouting, "I'm Soto! Come and get me! Buenos Noches Senors!"

The only man Pancho ever killed in his career of crime was a miner with whom he got into a dispute while at the New Almaden Mines. He later said he killed the man in self-defense.

A determined deputy sheriff named Patterson stuck on the trail of Soto until he caught up with the outlaw on Monterey Road. There a gunbattle raged, with Soto shooting Patterson in the leg, causing the deputy to fall off his horse.

Rather than fleeing, Pancho rode back to Patterson and wrapped the lawman's leg with his shirt, thus stopping the bleeding. He then went to the Twenty-One Mile House and told the innkeeper that a man was badly hurt up the road aways.

This action saved Patterson's life, although his leg had to be amputated. A short while later Pancho Soto was captured in San Jose. He was sentenced to life imprisonment but Deputy Sheriff Patterson went to Sacramento and told the Governor about how Pancho had helped him. Governor Booth granted Soto a full pardon in 1876.

A thankful ex-bandit went to work in the New Almaden Quicksilver Mines until he reached his late seventies. At this time he took on the easier job of cooking for the laborers at work on the structures of Lick Observatory on Mount Hamilton.

XLII

JUAN SOTO
A Worse Egg Could Not Be Found

Juan Soto was a bad egg—there are no two ways about it. Nobody knows what caused Juan to turn so bitter, but whatever it was it had a lasting effect. The Indian was a six-foot-two, 200-pound killer. Usually Soto did not even bother to rob his victims. The pleasure he got was in killing them in cold blood, seeing them beg for their lives, then die slowly and painfully.

Juan's crossed eyes and hardened face indicated his toughness: he was certainly no man to mess with. Somehow Juan got a group of cutthroats to ride with him, and together the merciless murderers "cut down" cattle, children, women, ministers, and all other types of men. While killing, it was said that Juan and his men never showed an expression on their stone faces.

Throughout the 1860's Juan Soto and his ruthless band terrorized Central and Northern California. Yet sheriff's posses could never track the outlaws, who always retreated through the rugged hills of the Coast Range.

Not only did Soto like to kill, but his second best lust was to burn—buildings, barns, fields, anything and everything he could set a match to.

It was January of 1871 when Juan's group rode into the small village of Sunol. After setting what buildings they could set on fire, Soto entered ex-Assemblyman Thomas Scott's store. Juan killed Scott's clerk, shot up everything in the store (barely missing Scott's wife and children, who were hiding in the back room), and set fire to the structure.

One of the largest manhunts in Northern California took place following this escapade. It was Sheriff Harris of Santa Clara and well-respected Alameda County Sheriff Harry Morse who got a tip on where Soto's killers were hiding.

Posses headed by these two men went up into the rugged area East of Pacheco Pass, near the Los Banos Creek. There

109

they were met by a sheepherder who was a good friend with both sheriffs. The sheepherder claimed to have accidentally spotted Soto's hideout, and he agreed to take the anxious lawmen to its vicinity in the Panoche Mountains.

The supposed hideout was an unguarded three-cabin complex. The two sheriffs split up the posses into three groups, one surrounding each cabin. As Morse and a deputy named Winchell advanced on one shack, a Mexican emerged from the door.

Morse quickly asked the man for a drink of water, and the two lawmen were invited inside. To the shock of Morse, sitting behind the door was Juan Soto, surrounded by seven men and two "Amazon" women.

When Sheriff Morse said, "You're all under arrest,'" the women jumped him, and the shotgun-wielding Deputy Winchell "took sick" at the sight of Soto and high-tailed it out the door, leaving the Sheriff to fend for himself.

Somehow Morse broke free and dove out the door. Meanwhile the posses surrounded the cabin, and there was no hope for Soto or his gang to escape. Juan made a dash for his horse, but was cut down by two bullets from Sheriff Morse's gun. Soto reportedly died with a look of utter disbelief on his ugly head. After all, his role was to kill, not to be killed.

XLIII

JAMES STUART
An Almost Fatal Case of Mistaken Identity

On February 19, 1851 San Francisco's Jansen, Bond and Company was robbed of $2,000. J. C. Jansen was beaten up. Before being taken to the hospital, Jansen told Sheriff Jack Hayes that the man who had pistol-whipped and robbed him was none other than the notorious James Stuart, widely known as the leader of the dreaded Sydney Town ruffians.

Within a week, Sheriff Hayes had what he thought to be his man. The suspect claimed his name was Thomas Berdue, and that he had never done a criminal act in his life.

Jansen identified Berdue as the culprit and several Sydney Towners agreed that it was indeed their leader in the pokey. One witness said it did not sound like Stuart; but he did have the split on his left ear lobe, the left forefinger was amputated at the first joint, and a small scar did appear over his left eye.

The lawabiding citizens of San Francisco shouted lynch, and handbills blanketed the city. "Addressed to the citizens of San Francisco: All those who would rid our city of its robbers and murderers will assemble at 2 o'clock on the plaza."

The newly formed vigilante committee ordered a trial, and Berdue was found to be guilty of assaulting and robbing Jansen. He was sentenced to fourteen years in prison, but before serving this sentence he had to be tried for the murder of Sheriff Moore, of Marysville, who had been killed by Stuart.

Sydney-towners were violently upset over what had happened to their leader. They retaliated by starting fires all over the city. Within half a day nearly three-forths of San Francisco had gone up in smoke. It was during these fires that Sheriff Hayes met an informant who claimed that James Stuart was "working" on the docks. Hayes left for the wharf and discovered the real James Stuart breaking into a captain's quarters aboard a vessel.

The vigilante committee met again on July 11, 1851 and found the real James Stuart guilty, and he was hanged that very day.

As for Thomas Berdue, he was brought back to San Francisco, given a parade in his honor, plus several thousand dollars for inconveniences brought on him, and then he disappeared an unobtrusive, thankful man.

XLIV

WILLIAM THORRINGTON and BILL EDWARDS
One Had Luck, the Other Took It

If the term "wheeler-dealer" could be tagged on a Utah territorian in the 1850's, Bill Thorrington of Genoa might very well have received the title. Not only did Bill control the profitable Carson Canyon Toll Road, but he was one of the select few who could bankrupt a gambling parlor. His luck at faro, roulette and poker was phenomenal, so much so that casino owners branded him, "Lucky Bill."

Bill and his wife and son also were successful cattle ranchers and had a several thousand acre spread. Therefore it was indeed puzzling as to why this fortunate character became involved with criminals. Perhaps it was a challenge to his clever mind to see if he could get away with anything, but whatever the reason, Bill Thorrington agreed to harbor a killer named Bill Combs Edwards.

Edwards most recent victim was a William B. Snelling, whom he gunned down in Merced County, California on December 4, 1857. Thorrington not only took Edwards into his home, but he made him a business partner and told Edwards to increase the size of the Thorrington Cattle Ranch Holdings.

Edwards proved his efficiency by doubling the herd. In fact he got so good at rustling that he temporarily left Thorrington to start "his own" ranch in the Honey Lake region. Using the name Charles Combs, Edwards purchased a ranch near Honey Lake.

Meanwhile Snelling's fraternal order, Merced Lodge No. 176, F. & A. M., offered a $1,500 reward for the capture of Edwards. A friend of Snellings, who also happened to be the neighbor of "Combs," thought the "Wanted" poster fit Charles to the letter, and the alert rancher rode into Merced to tell the Sheriff.

Edwards was tipped off about this action by a friend in Merced and he returned to "Lucky Bill's" ranch. He told Bill about a man he had seen who was driving a herd of cattle along the Truckee River in California.

113

Thorrington suggested that Edwards kill the man, draw up a forged bill of sale, and spread the word about that the Frenchman had gone back to France. Although he took no physical part in the crime, "Lucky Bill" was seen by a stagedriver talking to the Frenchman named Henry Gordier.

Everything worked out fine until Gordier's body was found by a rancher in a thick grove of trees near the river. A vigilante posse formed and rode out to Thorrington's Ranch. Both Bill and his sixteen-year-old son Jerome were taken into custody, but Edwards was not to be found.

Using an old trick, the vigilantes told Jerome that both he and his father would be set free if Edwards was captured. Jerome agreed to take them to Edwards hiding place. The young lad led the posse to a cabin hidden among the brush at the base of the Carson River. The vigilantes quietly surrounded the cabin, but Edwards had not returned for the evening.

The posse waited inside; and when Edwards returned home after midnight he was clubbed on the head and taken back to Honey Lake where he was subsequently hanged.

"Lucky Bill" was tried on June 19, 1858 and found to be guilty of being an accessory after the fact to the murder of Gordier. The eighteen-man jury declared that Thorrington was to be hanged that noon. The gallows were being erected during the course of the trial.

"Lucky Bill's" luck ran out at the old Clear Creek Ranch at the junction of the Carson and Eagle Valleys. His last words, as the noose was being fitted around his neck, were, "If you want to hang me, I'm no hog."

Thus ended the career of a once-lucky man who killed the golden goose by associating with a bad egg.

XLV

FRANK VALE
He Slept on His Partners' Graves

One of the weirdest and mentally unbalanced of Nevada's badmen was Frank Vale. Throughout his fifteen-year career of skulduggery, Vale, alias L. B. Vail, made friends and killed them just as fast.

From the Reese River South to the Pahranagat Valley, Vale terrorized ranchers by helping himself to horses and cattle after killing, burning and looting. His partners in crime did not last long, however, because following each job Vale would kill them. One historian says that Vale "delighted in the playful pastime of killing his associates and then sleeping on their graves."

Posses in search of the killer would find burial grounds around Vale's campsite; but the outlaw would always keep one step ahead of them. Finally, after months of frustration, lawmen got the break they were waiting for from an Indian squaw.

In Hiko, Nevada, a squaw's dog dug up the remains of Robert Knox—Vale's most recent partner. The squaw reported the find to a local Sheriff who tracked Vale to Austin, where the killer was arrested in a saloon without a fight.

While the Austin jurors sat listening to the legal jargon of a trial, others were outside building gallows and a coffin. Needless to say, Frank Vale was found guilty, hanged and buried, all in the same day. Ranchers definitely slept better that night knowing that the psycopathic robber-killer was no longer roaming the countryside.

XLVI

JEAN MARIE VILLEIAN
A Real Jack the Ripper

Preying on defenseless harlots must have made Jean Marie Villeian feel like a big man. The little Frenchman, who spoke no English, specialized in robbing prostitutes of all they had.

If the ladies of ill repute refused to give him whatever he wanted, Jean would beat them until they did. Despite his frequency of rape, robbery and sometimes murder, Villeian always managed to escape as he would travel from city to city in his gutless ventures.

Becoming increasingly proficient, cocky Jean Marie decided to branch upward and prey on the more successful ladies of easy virtue. This is where he made his mistake.

On January 19, 1867, Jean entered the D Street parlor of Julia Bulette, Queen of Comstock harlots. Julia was far more than just an ordinary prostitute. She was loved by the males of Virginia City because she often took care of sick miners, bought down and out prospectors meals, contributed to charity, comforted women and children during mine disasters, fought fires alongside men, and during a Paiute attack, was the only woman who refused to seek safety, preferring to stay with the men and bandage their wounds.

Naturally when Jean started robbing Julia, she put up quite a resistance. For her effort she was shot in the head, hit repeatedly with a log and gouged by her attackers long fingernails—but still she fought on. Finally, after having her head smashed violently against the bedboard, Julia Bulette "passed beyond the sunset."

Villeian left with Julia's valuables, but he had already committed his fatal mistake. The next morning, Julia's friend, Gertrude Holmes, discovered the ghastly body. Miss Bulette's head was smashed in, her bedclothes were drenched in blood, and her nude body revealed numerous slits cut by her killer's nails. The Territorial Enterprise called it, "The most cruel and outrageous and revolting murder ever committed in this city."

116

Police Chief W. E. Edwards and his men were frustrated because they could find no clues as to who the murderer was. Meanwhile one of the finest funerals in Comstock history sent Julia to her grave. Virginia City Engine Company Number One, of which Julia had been a member, provided the music for the parade thanking the gallant woman for what she had given to Virginia City.

Still not a trace of the killer turned up. Then on May 2 Martha Crump scared off a prowler after getting a good look at his face. Shortly after, Police Chief Edwards arrested Jean Villeian. At this time a woman in Gold Hill reported that Jean sold her some of Julia's dresses; and the Police Chief uncovered Miss Bulette's trunk in a bakery on D Street where Jean left it for safe keeping.

The May 24, 1867 Territorial Enterprise declared, "Nothing that has occured of late has created so profound a sensation among all classes of citizens as the discovery of the murderer of Julia Bulette."

On June 26, 1868 Jean Marie Valleian was tried under the name of John Villeian in Judge Richard Rising's court. A first degree murder decision was rendered by the biased jury. Jean was sentenced to be hanged.

Throngs of the populace stood on both sides of the street and on rooftops to get a good view of the gallows where Jean Villeian was rightfully hanged on April 24, 1868.

The harlots of the Comstock certainly slept a little easier that night, knowing that the man out to get them had gotten his.

XLVII

ELLA WATSON
She Took Her Wages in Cattle

Back in 1890 there was a much-used ice house in Sweet-water, Wyoming. However, not many people gave much thought to the history of the structure that had played a very controversial role a few years earlier.

The building was owned by James Averill, a Cornell University literature graduate who stood up for the small cattle ranchers in their constant struggles with the cattle barons. He often wrote letters to newspapers accusing the cattle barons of trying to monopolize land in the public domain, and of cutting off settlers' water rights.

One such letter appeared in the *Casper Weekly Mail*. In part, it read, "The big ranchers are opposed to anything that would settle and improve the country or make it anything but a cow pasture for eastern speculators."

For his crusading efforts, Averill was very popular with small ranchers; and his saloon was "the" spot to stop and have a snort in Sweetwater.

But one thing that seemed to be lacking from Averill's saloon was women, so he decided to have a female friend from Rawlins come and entertain the men in 1888.

The woman was twenty-six-year-old Ella Watson who was described by a Cheyenne paper as being robust, "a dark devil in the saddle, handy with a six-shooter and a Winchester, and an expert with a branding iron."

Needless to say, Miss Watson was an overnight success with the Sweetwater cattlemen, who came in droves to visit her in Averill's house.

The easy-going, good-humored woman was so popular that the men started meeting her fee by giving Ella cattle which were put in a large corral beside her business residence. Miss Watson's home was filled with antiques, and her corral was always packed with cattle—many of which were brought to her by rustlers in need of her services.

Still Ella's business prospered, and she reportedly had

dresses imported from Europe. In fact, things were going so well that she brought in another lady of easy virtue from Cheyenne.

Meanwhile, the large Wyoming cattle barons were getting upset with the increasing loss of their cattle, and through investigations they discovered many of the 'stray' animals in Ella's corral.

One cold December morning, a band of thirty cattlemen from the large ranches paid Miss Watson a visit. However, instead of bringing cattle—as her other customers did—they brought rifles.

Upon seeing the crowd of strangers in front of her home, Ella tried to slip out the back door. But the building was surrounded, and she was placed under vigilante custody in a freight wagon.

Ten of the cowboys turned Ella's cattle loose and drove them back to their rightful owners, while the other cattleman went to Averill's saloon, where he was wetting his whistle with a dozen of his men.

Outnumbered and caught by surprise, Averill threw down his gunbelt and boarded the wagon alongside his graciously-endowed female associate. As the cattleman began taking their prisoners toward the Sweetwater River, two of Averill's men rode to the ranch to inform their foreman, Frank Buchanan, of the kidnapping.

At the river the posse threatened to throw Miss Watson into the water if she would not confess to receiving stolen cattle. She reportedly laughed and joked that the water wasn't even deep enough to cleanse an old hog. The vigilantes started to throw Ella into the river when Frank Buchanan and five of Averill's men arrived at the scene and began shooting.

After an hour's fight, which left four men, two on each side, wounded, Buchanan, who was out of ammunition, was forced to surrender. Then a mock trial took place, and the jury declared Averill and Ella guilty of accepting stolen cattle.

Ropes were placed around both defendant's heads, and

119

they were pushed off boulders to meet their makers. The two painfully paid for their sins because the executioners had not tied the lynch knots correctly, and it was some time before Jim and Ella choked to death.

The six cattlemen most responsible for the incident were arrested the next day by the sheriff. They were A. Bothwell, R. Galbraith, Bob Conner, T. Sun, John Durbin, and E. McClain.

The Grand Jury of Carbon County met on Oct. 4, 1889, but failed to produce an indictment and the defendents were discharged.

Wrote the *Bessemer Journal* on Aug. 1, 1889: "It seems that the trouble which led to the crime was not cattle stealing, but grew out of land difficulties. We have heard parties say that they would wager their last dollar that Jim did not own a hoof; as for Ella, it is said she told the mob that if they would take her to Rawlins she would prove to them that she came by every head honestly and could show a bill of sale for each critter she owned or branded."

The Denver Republican editorialized on July 27, 1889: "Regardless of what the character of Jim and his mistress, the act of killing them was murder . . . The fact that the men who lynched them were, if such be the case, prominent citizens and respected does not excuse them . . . Wyoming is disgraced by this lynching."

Ironically, Jim and Ella's lavish, palacial residence was purchased by the leader of the vigilante cattlemen, who turned the former hot spot into a very cold ice house.

XLVIII

WILLIAM WILLIS
He Was a Burning Sensation

Firemen played a very vital role in wooden mining camps throughout the west in the nineteenth century. It was so easy for a horse to kick over a lantern or grease from an early-day stove, or a spark from a blacksmith's coals to start a blaze that would level half—or in many cases, the whole town.

If it was a prosperous diggings the miners would start rebuilding their town the next day. If the village was on a tailspin, miners would move off to a nearby town—turning their former residence into a ghost.

With fires proving such a great hazard, towns heavily relied on their fire departments, most of whom were volunteer.

In the famed camp of Virginia City, Nevada, members of the fire companies were looked upon as leaders in their communities; and each company had a band which performed during frequent parades and celebrations.

In 1871, one of Virginia City's finest firemen, who had saved several lives and structures through his heroic deeds, was young William Willis.

Willis, when he was not fighting fires as a member of Engine Company No. 4, was a carpenter who helped rebuild structures after fires.

The muscular man's talents were of particular importance in March of 1871, when a series of fires rocked Virginia City, leveling a couple of the town's most used public halls.

The fireman had to rely on ax work—because of a limited water supply—in order to contain the fires, which apparently were deliberately set.

Often firemen would be injured, and Willis was frequently treated for smoke inhalation and lacerations. During the Athletic Hall blaze, Willis received a fractured left arm, but he valiantly continued fighting the fire.

121

Fire Chief D. Downey conducted an investigation of every fire, but he could not locate the man responsible for tossing coal oil and matches on the buildings.

On March 13, two miners walking down E Street discovered flames in the rear of the famed Piper's Opera House. The alarm was given, and soon Virginia City's fire companies were on the scene.

Once again Downey blamed the cause of the fire on coal oil, which saturated lumber in the rear of the old structure. Downey and sheriff's deputies began a search for a person or persons having oil on their clothes.

The exhaustive search ended in the office of Company No. 4, where Downey located a coat belonging to Willis, which had oil soaked on its arm sleeves.

Downey arrested Willis after the fireman returned from mop-up operations at the Opera House. On Willis' trousers were dust particles matching those found on the lumber where the fire had started.

Downey was also able to come up with two witnesses who had seen Willis standing, watching the blaze get started across from the Opera House.

An enraged vigilante committee took Willis from Downey's custody and threatened to hang him if he did not confess to the rash of fires.

Willis reportedly told the mob that he had started several of the fires because he liked the attention he got for his valor in putting them out.

The sick fireman also named three other men who had borrowed coal oil from him to start other blazes. The vigilantes turned Willis over to the sheriff, and he was later sentenced to twenty years in the Nevada State Penitentiary at Carson City.

Willis was never heard from again, much to the relief of Virginia Citians.

XLIX

JUANITA X
Her Temper Stretched Her Neck

On the day of July 4, 1851 the diggin's of Downieville, California was in a joyous uproar. Everyone was happy, picnics and parades entertained the women and children, and the saloons catered to the men's desires. Miners took turns "buying the house" drinks, and the dance hall girls dealt cards while the piano belted out a fast-paced tune.

Charley Lawson and his mining partner, Jock Cannon were treating the Jack Craycroft Saloon patrons to round after round of refreshment. Soon Cannon was drunk and decided to sit down and attempt to play poker. He chose the table operated by a dance hall beauty named Juanita X.

Major William Downie described Juanita as a woman of "Spanish-Mexican mixture, and the blood of her fathers flowed fast and warmly in her veins. She was proud, and self-possessed, and her bearing was graceful, almost majestic. She was, in the miners' parlance, 'well put up.' Her figure was richly developed and in strict proportions; her features delicate, and her olive complexion lent them a pleasing softness. Her black hair was neatly done up on state occasions and the lustre in her eyes shone in various degrees, from the soft-like expression of a love-sick maiden, to the fierce scowl of an infuriated lioness, according to her temper, which was the only thing not well balanced about her."

Naturally when the obnoxious Cannon reached over and grabbed Juanita, she withdrew, pulling a knife from inside her low-cut blouse. Jock backed off and nothing more was thought about the matter, until Cannon and Lawson wobbled their way home early the next morning.

In an act of anger and revenge, Cannon decided to kick down Juanita's door as they passed her cabin, but he did not proceed inside because Lawson pulled his drunk partner home.

Later that morning, after they sobered up a bit, Cannon

and Lawson felt a bit guilty and Cannon went back to Juanita's cabin to apologize. Juanita, outraged to say the least, grabbed her stiletto and plunged it deep into Cannon—or so one version of the story goes. The other version says that Cannon entered Juanita's cabin to make a pass at her, and Miss X knifed him in self-defense.

Anyway, a make shift mob formed and declared Juanita X guilty of murder, and she was sentenced to hang. The jury disregarded a physician's evidence stating that Juanita was pregnant, and they ordered the doctor to leave town.

That afternoon, before 2,500 men, women and children, Juanita X was hanged near a bridge in Downieville, making her the first and last woman to ever be hanged in a Mother Lode Camp. The press debated the hanging for several weeks.

The Sonora Union Democrat editor believed that Juanita was acting in self-defense. "At Downieville was perpetrated the greatest possible crime against humanity, Christianity, and civilization. A drunken gambler, with criminal audacity, had thrust himself into the presence of a Spanish woman of doubtful character.

"She was [pregnant]; enraged at his demeamor she seized a knife in a moment of passion, thrust it into his breast and killed him. The gambler was popular, as gamblers may be and as many are. The mob, in angry excitement, seized the poor, trembling, wretched woman, tried, convicted and hanged her; hanged her in spite of her situation, her entreaties, and the fact that she killed her assailant in defense of her person."

This editor's belief was in the minority, however, and most felt Juanita X to be guilty of murder. The San Francisco Alta correspondent wrote a "Majority" opinion. At the trial, "The people did not 'by vote' order Dr. Aiken to leave town because he declared the woman to be [pregnant], but because they believed his object was to screen her from justice.

"The victim in this instance was not the first nor the second who had been stabbed by the same female . . . I have lived long enough in Downieville to know that its inhabitants are not the blood-thirsty, diabolical monsters they have been represented; on the contrary, they have heretofore been too mild in their punishment of offenders; and in the case before us, nothing induced them to pursue the course they did but retributive justice."

L

CONVICT LAKE
The Prison Break That Renamed a Lake

Editor's Note: No book on desperadoes would be complete without the story of the greatest prison break—engineered by twenty-nine desperate outlaws in 1871. The badmen involved in the escape were not the infamous outlaws of the west, but a group of nobodys who banded together for one purpose—to escape. It should be remembered that Jack Davis, stage and train robber, helped officials collar several convicts before they were able to escape, and thus received a Governor's full pardon for his heroic actions.

As the sun slipped beneath the rugged slopes of the Sierras, a flurry of activity took place behind the cell walls of the Nevada State Penitentiary in Carson City, Nevada. It was the night of September 17, 1871—an evening of hope for twenty-nine convicts.

The desperate prisoners culminated months of tedious planning by luring the captain of the guard to one of the cells. As Volney E. Rollins, the chief sentry, cautiously peered through the cold steel bars to inquire about a sick inmate's groans, he was grabbed by the collars, pulled against the bars, and hit over the head with a bottle.

After being gagged, the guard's keys were taken off and he became the means by which the freedom-hungry prisoners could escape. Thus began a series of events which would develop into one of the greatest manhunts in history, and which would change the name of California's Monte Diablo Lake to Convict Lake.

Using the head guard as hostage, the convicts opened several other cells before guiding their helpless victim to the warden's quarters. In the prison official's office they confronted the warden and visiting Lieutenant Governor Frank Denver.

As an early journalist recorded: "Denver met the mob at the door. Frank Clifford, a horse-thief doing 17 years, was in the lead. Denver emptied a pistol at him before being prostrated by a shower of blows.

"Most of the guards were off duty. One named Isaacs faced the escapees as they neared the outer door of the building, and shot at them as long as he had a round left. Some of the convicts were able to seize rifles from the armory and they returned Isaac's fire. A bullet broke his right leg at the knee, but he managed to stand on one leg and oppose them. Another shot broke his hip and he fell.

"In admiration for his courage his life was spared."

The motley crew grabbed Denver and Isaacs and made their way to the front gate, where several officers were just returning from a night on the town.

Near the gate, the guards, unaware of the hostages, opened fire on the group of convicts. A gun battle, which left two guards dead and several on both sides injured, continued until the hostages yelled out for recognition.

Meanwhile, Matt Pixley, a hotel keeper, ran into the yard with his gun drawn, and was promptly shot through the head by the escapees.

The convicts next ordered horses, which they exchanged for the lives of the hostages.

Once outside the prison walls, the murderers, train robbers and horse thieves scattered in all directions, heading toward Reno, Pioche, Owens Valley and Beatty. Once word of the jailbreak reached Carson City, two units of the state militia, and posses totaling nearly 300 men were hastily organized and sent out in search of the wayward men.

The states of Nevada and California were warned via circulars that extreme caution must be exercised when dealing with the criminals, since it was known they were well armed with sixshooters, shotguns, Henry rifles, plus ample ammunition to raise large-scale havoc.

Six of the figitives headed for the Monte Diablo Lake region in the eastern High Sierras, thus bringing about California's involvement in the episode.

The six—Fred Jones, a murderer; Chafin Cockerill, an ex-Army officer and train robber; Moses Black, a horse thief; John Burke, a murderer; Jim Roberts, a stage robber; and Leander Morton, a killer and leader of the prison break—all knew the Sierra terrain quite well.

127

Destined for Owens Valley, they had hoped to encounter Captain William Dingman. USA, Ret., then a mail rider, who, as a prison guard killed two convicts during an earlier escape attempt.

Unfortunately for the escapees, they met William A. Poor, a popular mail rider, and the convicts made a fatal mistake by killing the youngster. Jones donned the young man's clothes and carelessly left his prison blues behind.

When Billy did not arrive at Bishop on schedule, the Sacramento Union editorialized that he would be found dead, a victim of the escapees. Sure enough, such was the case. The brutal murder gave the posse added incentive to find the killers.

Deputy Sheriff George Hightower, a close friend of Billy's, led a search party of a dozen men to Monte Diablo Canyon. It was there that lawmen located Jones' prison clothes, picked up the convict's trail, and followed them deep into the canyon.

As the law neared the south end of the lake, the convicts, hidden behind a large grove of pine and willow trees, opened fire, ambushing the posse. A rip-roaring shoot-out lasted throughout the afternoon of September 24. Several men from both sides were injured, two lawmen were killed. One of the fatalities, Robert Morrison, was a prominent Wells Fargo agent who had volunteered to track the outlaws. Today, 12,268-foot Mount Morrison, named in honor of Robert, stands at the south end of the lake.

Jones, Burke, and Cockerill, who were out of camp during the fight, remained in hiding and were not located by the posse.

Eventually the much-wounded posse limped back to Bishop, where a larger group of vigilantes took over the chase. Lead by John Crough and John Clarke, and aided by local militiamen, the fresh hunting party left in pursuit of the elusive convicts.

The determined posse easily located Black and Morton, who had foolishly left their well-hidden hideaway. Two

John and Charles Ruggles were unsuccessful robbers. For their efforts they were hanged in Redding, California.

Milton Sharp was a distinguished gentleman who had only one bad habit—he robbed stages.

Juan Soto terrorized Central and Northern California in the 1860's.
Courtesy of the Wells Fargo History Room.

Courageous Sheriff Harry Morse put an end to Juan Soto's bloody career with two well-positioned bullets.

Julia Bulette, of infamous reputation in Virginia City, Nevada, was brutally murdered on January 19, 1867.

Courtesy of the Bucket of Blood Saloon, Virginia City, Nevada.

Jean Villeian specialized in robbing harlots. His fatal mistake came when he killed the well-liked Julia Bulette.

Prison escapees ambushed the Sheriff's posse at this lake, which therefore became known as "Convict Lake."   Author's Collection.

WELLS, FARGO & CO.'S EXPRESS
STAGE ROBBERY REPORT.

Candelaria Nevada Dec. 11-82

The Stage bound from _Candelaria_

to _Columbus_ was robbed

about 9 o'clock A. M., _Dec 6th_, 18 8 2. 3 miles from

Columbus in _Esmeralda_ County,

Nev., by 1 man, armed with _Rifle_

and disguised with _sacks_

on head "us feet —

Name of driver _Samuel S. Farmon_

Mails _not_ taken and

Wells, Fargo & Co.'s loss _Nothing_

Amount recovered _____

Names, residences, and losses of passengers:

No passengers.

E B Cushman
Agent W F & Co.
Candelaria Nev.

(OVER.)

WELLS FARGO BANK

Wells Fargo Stage Robbery Report. Wells Fargo
agents became very familiar with this form in the
nineteenth century, when large shipments of gold
and valuables were frequently held up.

A SPECULATOR.

This is supposedly a likeness of swindler Frank Phillips, who became a victim of fellow outlaw Sheet-Iron Jack. Courtesy of *Harpers Magazine*, June 1862.

Simone Jules. "Madame Moustache" defends herself from two robbers in Bodie, California. Courtesy of the Denver Public Library, Western Collection.

Thomas Bell Poole was hanged on this street in Placerville, California.

Courtesy of the California State Library.

This scene in the Sierras is near Bullion Bend, where Confederate Robin Hoods scored one of the largest holdups in the Far West. Courtesy of the Bancroft Library.

Cattlerustler Susan Raper often watered her herds in Churchill County's Humboldt River.

Courtesy of the Nevada Historical Society.

Outlaws kept a close watch on the National Hotel in Nevada City, California, where some of the richest men in the Mother Lode stayed. It was not uncommon for wealthy miners who stayed there to become victims in a holdup.

Photo by David Hillman.

California highwaymen often hid their loot in mineshafts like this one near Grass Valley, California.   Photo by David Hillman.

Dr. Yee's Herb Shop in Fiddletown, California, now a gold rush museum, shows the precautions Mother Lode merchants took against burglary. Note caged windows, iron window shutters, and bars on doors. Photo by David Hillman.

days later, Roberts was also taken prisoner in Round Valley. Roberts reportedly begged for food, saying that he had not eaten in five days.

The three outlaws were taken from the law-minded vigilantes by a group of outraged citizens in Bishop. Black and Morton were hanged by the same rope, but young Roberts was allowed to return to the penitentiary.

Burke and Cockerill were later rounded up by militiamen in Southeastern Nevada, Jones was never recaptured.

Meanwhile, the militiamen and posses recaptured eight and killed fifteen of the escapees in gunfights. The remaining five were arrested outside of Nevada.

This massive prison break caused the state of Nevada to hire James B. Hume, former Sheriff of El Dorado County, to shape up the Nevada Penitentiary so as to prevent such a thing from recurring.

Because of the manhunt and ambush, the lake, stream and canyon were renamed Convict, instead of Monte Diablo, by local citizens—an official name change that remains with us today.

Now Convict Lake, 39 miles north of Bishop, just off of U.S. Highway 395, is a favorite stomping grounds for campers, fishermen, backpackers, horseback riders, geology buffs, and gold panners—a spot rich in sport and history.

APPENDIX A

The Crime and Punishment Report of Wells Fargo

(Report of Jas. B. Hume and Jno. N. Thacker, special officers, Wells Fargo & Co's Express, covering a period of 14 years, giving losses by Stage Robbers, Train Bandits and Burglaries, and a description and record of all noted criminals, convicted of offenses against Wells Fargo and Company from November 5, 1870 to November 5, 1884. San Francisco: H. S. Crocker & Co., Stationers and Printers, 1885.)

Mr. Jno. J. Valentine, Vice Pres. and Gen'l Manager of Wells Fargo & Company, San Francisco.

Dear Sir:

We have compiled from the records in our Department the following data, extending over a fourteen year period—from November 5th, 1870, to November 5, 1884. The amounts taken, attendant expenses, pay of guards and special officers, may not be exact, but are not overstated. The data giving the number and character of offenses committed, names of offenders, the number of convictions secured, lives lost, etc., etc., are substantially correct.

Total amount taken from W. F. & Co's Express by stage robbers, train robbers and burglars during fourteen years beginning November 5, 1870	$415,312.55
Rewards paid for arrest and conviction of said robbers, etc. and percentage paid on treasure recovered	73,451.00
Attorney's fees and legal expenses of prosecution	22,367.00
Incidental expenses incurred in arrests and convictions	90,079.00
Salary of guards and special officers	326,517.00
Total Loss	927,726.55
Number of Stage Robberies during the fourteen years above named	313
Number of Attempted Stage Robberies	34

Number of Burglaries	23
Number of Train Robberies	4
Number of Attempted Train Robberies	4
Number of Convictions for Robbery and attempt at stage robbery	206
Number of Convictions for Train Robbery and attempt at same	20
Number of Convictions for Burglary	14

Number of W. F. & Co's Guards killed in discharge of duty, by stage robbers   2

Andy Hall, August 20, 1882, on route to Globe, A. T. (Arizona Territory)

John H. Collins, August 10, 1883 on route Florence to Globe, A. T.

Number of W. F. & Co's Guards wounded while in discharge of duty, by stage and train robbers   6

James Miller, December 3, 1874, on route Eureka to Palisade, Nev.

Jimmy Brown, September 3, 1877, on route Eureka to Tybo, Nevada.

Wm. Blankenship, July, 1879, on route Maricopa to Phoenix, A. T.

Mike Tovey, September 5, 1880, on route Bodie to Carson, Nevada.

George W. Hackett, July 13, 1882, on route Laporte to Oroville, Calif.

A. Y. Ross, January 22, 1883, on route San Francisco to Ogden (train) (Utah Territory)

Number of Stage Drivers killed by robbers during the fourteen years.   4

Billy Mann, April 27, 1873, on route Hamilton to Pioche, Nev.

Charlie Phelps, July 30, 1883, on route Corinne, U. T., to Montana.

Budd (Eli) Philpot, March 15, 1881, on route Tombstone to Benson (A. T.)

Señor Romero, July 19, 1884, on route Railroad Depot to Leone, Mex.

Number of Stage Drivers seriously wounded by robbers 4

L. C. Woodworth, February 17, 1871, on route Petaluma to Cloverdale.

Jerry Culverhouse, February 16, 1875, on route Shasta to Redding.

George H. Smith, March 9, 1877, on route Anaheim to San Diego.

Richard Richards, December 14, 1881, on route Tombstone to Benson.

Number of Passengers killed by stage robbers during the fourteen years 4

Henry P. Benton, February 17, 1871, on route Petaluma to Cloverdale.

John T. Lloyd, February 14, 1877, on route Mojave to Darwin.

Peter Roerig, March 15, 1881, on route Tombstone to Benson, A. T.

Dr. W. T. Vail, August 20, 1882, on route Florence to Globe, A. T.

Number of Passengers seriously wounded by stage robbers 2

A. Kaufman, February 17, 1871, on route Petaluma to Cloverdale.

Henry Scammon, November 13, 1876, on route Downieville to Marysville.

Number of Stage Robbers Killed while in the act of robbing or attempting to rob the express on stages, by W. F. & Co's guard 5

H. S. Hunt, by guard McNamara, Oct. 24, 1876, on route Weaver to Shasta.

John Carlo, by guard Eugene Blair, September 3, 1877, on route Eureka to Ward, Nev.

Jack Davis, by guards Jimmy Brown and Eugene Blair, September 3, 1877, on route Eureka to Tybo, Nev.

Andy Marsh, by guard J. E. Reynolds, September 7, 1878, on route Yreka to Redding.

W. C. Jones, alias Frank Dow, by guard Mike Tovey, September 5, 1880, on route Bodie to Carson.

Number of robbers killed while resisting arrest   11

Joe Brown, alias Foster, Nov. 18, 1876.

John Brazelton, August 19, 1878.

Jack Brown, alias O'Neil, April 26, 1881.

Harry Head, June 1, 1881.

Jack Almer, Oct. 3, 1883.

Joe Blanchard, July 18, 1877.

Thomas Francis, Nov. 19, 1879.

Bill Leonard, June 1, 1881.

Jim Crane, Oct. 3, 1882.

Chas. Hensley, Oct. 3, 1883.

George W. Cleveland, March 10, 1884.

Number of Robbers hanged by citizens in the fourteen years   7

Leander Morton, near Aurora, Nev., Sept. 27, 1871.

C. B. Hawley, Globe, A. T., Aug. 25, 1882

Joe Tuttle, Florence, A. T., Sept. 3, 1883.

Frank Taggart, Silver City, N. M., March 10, 1884.

Lafayette Grimes, Globe, A. T., Aug. 25, 1882.

Len Redfield, Florence, A. T., Sept. 3, 1883.

Mitch Lee, Silver City, N. M., March 10, 1884

You will notice by the foregoing that the number of lives lost, as the result of the above enumerated robberies and attempted robberies, amounts to thirty three.

There have been seven horses killed, and thirteen stolen from the various stage teams in time of robberies and attempted robberies during the fourteen years in our report.

Your attention is invited to the details connected with these extensive operations, which follow this summary.

Respectfully submitted,

J. B. Hume

J. N. Thacker

Special Officers

San Francisco, December 19, 1884.

APPENDIX B

THE BALLAD OF BALDY GREEN

This poem was composed in the 1860's, soon after Baldy Green, famed stagewhip from Virginia City, was held up.

I'll tell you all a story,
   And I'll tell it in a song,
And I hope that it will please you,
   For it won't detain you long.

'Tis about one of the old boys
   So gallus and so fine,
Who used to carry mails
   On the Pioneer Line.

He was the greatest favor-ite
   That ever yet was seen,
He was known about Virginny
   By the name of Baldy Green.

Oh, he swung a whip so gracefully,
   For he was bound to shine—
For he was a high-toned driver
   On the Pioneer Line.

Now, as he was driving out one night,
   As lively as a coon,
He saw three men jump in the road
   By the pale light of the moon.

Two sprang for the leaders,
   While one his shotgun cocks,
Saying, "Baldy, we hate to trouble you,
   But just pass us out the box."

When Baldy heard them say these words
   He opened wide his eyes,
He didn't know what in the world to do
   For it took him by surprise.

Then he reached into the boot,
   Saying, "Take it, sirs, with pleasure,"
So out into the middle of the road
   Went Wells Fargo's treasure.

Now, when they got the treasure box
   They seemed quite satisfied,
For the man who held the leaders
   Then politely stepped aside.

Saying, "Baldy, we've got what we want,
   So drive along your team,"
And he made the quickest time
   To Silver City ever seen.

Don't say greenbacks to Baldy now,
   It makes him feel so sore;
He'd traveled the road many a time,
   But was never stopped before.

Oh, the chances they were three to one
   And shotguns were the game,
And if you'd a-been in Baldy's place,
   You'd a-shelled her out the same.

APPENDIX C

DESPERADO TERMS AND PHRASES

Cashed in his chips—When the outlaw died. Other phrases: *met his maker, bit the dust, passed beyond the sunset, gone over the divide, folded up his tent, drew to the spade,* and *turned on his back.*

Change room—The place where miners changed into their street clothes. It was created by mine owners to catch laborers who smuggled ore out in their bulky work clothes.

Coachman—The admired stage driver. Also called *whip, Jehu,* and *Charley.*

Coast is clear—Expression whereby a lookout signaled to fellow outlaws that they could continue their illegal actions without interference, especially from the law.

Cowboy—One who works on cattle grazing land. Also called *puncher, cowpoke, waddy, wrangler.*

Desperado—A bold, reckless criminal with "a light hand for other people's property." Also known as *a bad egg.*

Getting drilled—Being shot. Also called *being done in, payed a visit, stung by a rattle of lead.*

Got wind of—When an outlaw heard some information which aided his career, either by helping him to escape or by showing him where some money was.

Harlot—A female prostitute. Also called *princess of a sin emporium, crib lady, woman of easy virtue, lady of ill-repute.*

Hell-bent for action—Having a good, carefree time. Other such phrases: *rip roarin', rootin' tootin' ripsnorter, footloose and fancy free.* On occasion the defined phrase has also referred to the state of being determined to seek revenge at any cost.

High-tailed it—Moved rapidly, usually to get away from the law.

Ironed him—When a sheriff put handcuffs on his prisoner.

Jawing—Talking. Also called *yapping, spinning some yarns which was raisin' 'em out of their boots.*

137

Leaders—The two front horses in a team of four or six horses which pull stages. These horses could be grabbed by highwaymen to insure that the stage would stop.

Leather 'n lead—The desperado who often possessed *leather gear* (holster, chaps, vest, saddle) and had the ability to draw quickly and *spit lead* (shoot bullets) on the mark.

Pokey—A room of confinement for lawbreakers. Better known as *jail*.

Road agent—One who robs people. Also called *highwayman, bandit*.

Seeing the elephant—Searching for gold; going through a trying and unpleasant experience and getting the best of it, or at least coming out alive.

Shotgun—The guard or messenger who sits with a shotgun weapon by the whip, and is responsible for the safety of the stage's cargo.

Sizing his pile—Betting in a poker game.

Spilled the beans—Letting something slip out that is not supposed to.

Water your whistle—Taking a *slug* (drink) of whiskey. Other like phrases: *getting high in spirits, grabbing a couple of snorts, kicking 'em down like a mule*.

APPENDIX D

DESPERADO EPITAPHS

The Western desperado sent many people to an early grave but eventually justice caught up with him. As William Raine wrote in *Guns of the Frontier*, "The killer had his day, then came to a swift and violent end. There were exceptions, but so few as to emphasize the rule. If the law did not get them, another bad man did."

Following are epitaphs paying tribute to several desperadoes, many of whom met a violent death.

GUNFIGHTER (Tombstone, Arizona)
    Here Lies Lester Moore
    Four Slugs From A .44
    No Les
    No More.

CONMAN (Denver, Colorado)
    Here Lies Big Bill
    He Always Lied
    And Always Will;
    He Once Lied Loud
    He Now Lies Still.

THIEF AND DRUNK (Los Angeles, California)
    Here Lies Allan None
    He Might Be Here Today
    But Bum Whiskey And A
    Bad Gun Put Him Away.

HORSE THIEVES (Rapid City, South Dakota)

HORSE THIEVES BEWARE

Here Lies The Body Of Allen, Curry And Hall
Like Other Thieves They Had Their Rise, Decline And Fall;
On Yon Pine Tree They Hung Till Dead
And Here They Found A Lonely Bed.

Then Be A Little Cautious How You Gobble Horses Up
For Every Horse You Pick Up Here Adds Sorrow To Your Cup;
We're Bound To Stop This Business Or Hang You To A Man
For We've Hemp And Hands Enough In Town To Swing The Whole
    Damn Clan.

OUTLAW: CATTLE RUSTLER (Douglas, Wyoming)
    Underneath This Stone In Eternal Rest
    Sleeps The Wildest One Of The Wayward West
    He Was A Gambler And Sport And Cowboy Too
    And He Led The Pace In An Outlaw Crew.
    He Was Sure On The Trigger And Staid To The End
    But He Was Never Known To Quit On A Friend
    In The Relations Of Death All Mankind Is Alike
    But In Life There Was Only One George W. Pike.

DEBTOR (Dutch Flat, California)
    Owen Moore Has Gone Away
    Owin' More Than He Could Pay.

BULLY (Virginia City, Montana)
    Here Lies Pete
    With His Guts Full Of Lead
    He Was Only A Bag Of Wind
    And Now He Is Dead.

PROSTITUTE (Pioche, Nevada)
   Here Lies The Body Of Virginia Harlotte,
   She Was Born A Virgin And Died A Harlot.
   For Eighteen Years She Preserved Her Virginity—
   That's A Damned Good Record For This Vicinity.

HORSE THIEF (Carson City, Nevada)
   He Found A Rope And Picked It Up,
   And With It Walked Away.
   It Happened That To The Other End
   A Horse Was Hitched, They Say.
   They Took The Rope And Tied It Up
   Unto A Hickory Limb.
   It Happened That The Other End
   Was Somehow Hitched To Him.

GAMBLER (Virginia City, Nevada)
   This Is The Grave Of Timothy Tush
   He Drew On His Sleeve For A Royal Flush.

GUNFIGHTER (Silver City, Nevada)
   Here Lays Butch,
   We Planted Him Raw.
   He Was Quick On The Trigger
   But Slow On The Draw.

GUNFIGHTER (Skidoo, California)
   Here Lie The Remains Of Joshia Shuh
   Second-fastest Draw In Skidoo.

SUSPECTED BANKROBBER (Tombstone, Arizona)
   Here Lies A Man Who Was Named Curtis Ball,
   Who Lost His Life In A Short Fall.
   A Rope Was Around His Neck At The Time—
   That's All.

BIBLIOGRAPHY

Following is a selected bibliography of secondary sources and individuals interviewed during the research and writing of this manuscript.

Amador County History. Amador County Federation of Womens Clubs, April, 1927.

Angel, Myron, ed. *History of Nevada.* Thompson and West, 1881.

Arbuckle, Clyde. Santa Clara Valley historian.

Ashbough, Don. *Nevada's Turbulent Yesterday.* Los Angeles: Westernlore Press, 1963.

Banning, Captain William. *Sixhorses.* New York: Century & Co., 1928.

Bartholomew, ed. *Album of Western Gunfighters.* Houston: Frontier Press, 1958.

Beales, B.B. "San Jose and the Civil War." *California Historical Society Quarterly,* December, 1943.

Beebe, Lucius and Charles Clegg. *U. S. West: Saga of Wells Fargo.* New York: E. P. Dutton and Co., 1949.

Beebe. *Legends of the Comstock Lode.* Stanford University Press, 1950.

Bell, Major Horace. *Reminiscences of a Ranger.* 1881.

Block, Eugene. *Great Stagecoach Robbers of the West.* London: Alvin Redman, 1963.

Bulmore, Lawrence. New Almaden historian and author.

Caughey, John. *California.* New York: Prentice-Hall, 1970.

"Convict Lake," *Mineral Information Service Bulletin,* June, 1969.

Curtis, Mabel. Pajaro Valley historian and author.

Dillon, Richard. *Wells Fargo Detective.* New York: Coward-McCann, 1969.

Drury, Wells. *An Editor on the Comstock.* Palo Alto: Pacific Books, 1936.

Fisher, Vardis and Opal L. Holmes. *Gold Rushes and Mining Camps of the Early American West.* Caxton Printers, 1968.

Gehm, Katherine. *Nevada's Yesteryear.* Colorado: Filter Press, 1970.

Gilbert, Ben F. "The Confederate Minority in California." *California Historical Society Quarterly*, June, 1941.

Gilbert, Benjamin F. California historian and author.

Giles, Rosena A. *Shasta County*. Oakland: Biobooks, 1949.

Glasscock, C. B. *A Golden Highway*. New York: Blue Ribbon Books, 1941.

Harrison, E. S. *History of Santa Cruz County*. San Francisco: Pacific Press, 1892.

History of Nevada County. Oakland: Thompson and West, 1880.

History of Placer County. Oakland: Thompson and West, 1882.

History of Plumas, Lassen, and Sierra Counties. San Francisco: Fariss and Smith, 1882.

History of Yuba County. Oakland: Thompson and West, 1879.

Jackson, Joseph Henry. *Bad Company*. New York: Harcourt, Brace & Co., 1949.

Jackson. *Anybody's Gold*. San Francisco: Chronicle Books. Reprinted 1971.

James, William and George McMurray. *History of San Jose*. San Jose: A. H. Cawston, 1933.

Loomis, Noel M. *Wells Fargo*. New York: Potter, 1968.

Lyman, George D. *Saga of the Comstock Lode*. New York: Charles Scribner's Sons, 1934.

Martin, ed. *History of Santa Clara County*. Los Angeles: Historic Records Company, 1911.

Martin, ed. *History of Santa Cruz County*. Los Angeles: Historic Records Company, 1911.

Murbarger, Nell. *Ghosts of the Glory Trail*. Los Angeles: Westernlore, 1956.

Nelson, Frank and Kay. Longtime Santa Clara County cattlemen-ranchers.

Newmark, H. *Sixty Years in Southern California*. 1930.

Patterson, Edna B., Louise A. Ulph, Victor Goodwin, *Nevada's Northeast Frontier*. Western Publishing Company, 1969.

Pioneer Nevada Papers, Summerfield Room, University of Nevada, Reno.

Rambo, Ralph. *Almost Forgotten*. San Jose: Rosecrutian Press, 1964.

Riesenberg, Felix. *The Golden Road*. New York: McGraw-Hill, 1962.

Sawyer, Eugene. *History of Santa Clara County*. Los Angeles: Historic Records Co., 1922.

Sioli, Paolo. *Historical Souvenir of El Dorado County, California*. Oakland, 1883.

Smith, Grant H. *The History of the Comstock Lode*. Reno, 1943.

Swan, Oliver G. *Covered Wagon Days*. New York: Grosset and Dunlap, 1928.

"Three Notorious Bandits of the Fifties." *California Historical Society Quarterly*, December, 1943.

Wenger, Bob and Dorothy. Resort owners, Convict Lake.

Williams, Brad and Choral Pepper. *Lost Legends of the West*. New York: Holt, Rinehart and Winston, 1970.

Wilson, Neill. *Treasure Express*. New York: MacMillan, 1936.